Early Accolades for *Divine Wisdom at Work*™

"Great entrepreneurs often rely on their innate wisdom to make decisions and solve problems. This unique book presents a set of principles that turns common business challenges into valuable opportunities."
Charlie Goetz, CEO, Intelligent Medical Solutions, LLC, and Adjunct Professor of Entrepreneurship, Goizueta Graduate School of Business at Emory University

"Divine Wisdom at Work™ is a remarkable book. Tricia Molloy has taken spiritual principles and presented them in a real-world context. It will inspire even the most pragmatic leaders to see their power and their possibilities for producing extraordinary results."
Jim Huling, CEO, MATRIX Resources, Inc. and Author of the Nationally Syndicated Column, *The Business of Life*

"Divine Wisdom at Work™ is a brilliant, easy-to-read tutorial that can transform any business. Tricia Molloy has applied ten powerful principles to the business world using inspiring true stories, practical exercises and personal experiences."
Carole O'Connell, Unity North Minister Emerita and Author of *Ten Ways to Create a Joyous Life*

"Like the phenomenal bestseller, *The 7 Habits of Highly Effective People, Divine Wisdom at Work*™ provides an innovative and practical framework for those seeking to reach their highest potential. It shows entrepreneurs how to integrate proven spiritual principles with sound business practices."
Ken Menendez, Attorney and Author of *Taming the Lawyers*

"I've been a business owner since 1968. What impresses me most about *Divine Wisdom at Work*™ is the multitude of tangible examples that shows how each of these principles work. It's an enjoyable quick study for anyone contemplating going into business, as well as for business owners who are looking to try something new."
Eric Lindberg, President, Founder and CEO of MSI International

"This is a spirited business book with heart and soul. It will change the way you look at your work and your life."
Karen Drucker, Inspirational Singer/Songwriter

"Inspiring, yet practical. This is just what busy entrepreneurs need to joyfully embrace their own Divine Wisdom."
Susan Pilgrim, Ph.D., Author of *Living InSync*®—*Creating Your Life with Balance and Purpose*

"Tricia Molloy has written a timely, substantive book for business owners. Her refreshing insights and her prescription, if followed, will revitalize you and recharge your business."
Elizabeth Pagano, Co-Author of the *Fast Company* Magazine Readers' Choice Book, *The Transparency Edge: How Credibility Can Make or Break You in Business*

"Achieving balance is one of the most common challenges of entrepreneurs. Tricia Molloy has done a great job providing inspirational, as well as practical, ideas to help attain that balance."
Millann Funk, Publisher of *Serious About Small Business*

**10 Universal Principles for
Enlightened Entrepreneurs**

Tricia Molloy

DEDICATION

To the Divine Wisdom in me
that inspired the creation of this book,
and the Divine Wisdom in you
that guided you to it.

CONTENTS

WITH GRATITUDE

I was inspired to write *Divine Wisdom at Work*™ for many reasons. One was the vivid picture I purposely kept in my head of everyone who would read this book and apply these principles for extraordinary results. Another was my clear intention to promote this set of universal principles as a new business model by attracting like-minded clients for consulting and coaching services, audiences for my speeches, workshops and business classes, and partners for other books and projects.

As I finished writing this book, I discovered another reason. It was a rare opportunity to openly express in one place sincere appreciation to those who have had such a profound influence on my life. Their belief in me and my message has made all the difference.

To my parents, Lorraine and James Molloy, for always encouraging me as a writer and seeing "our daughter, the author" way before it was official. Special thanks to my sister, Susan Molloy Familia, for her love and support.

To my seventh-grade English teacher, Ms. Coughlin, for persuading me to submit a few of my poems to our school paper when I was 12 years old. She gifted me with the joy of seeing my words publicly in print for the first time. That's when I knew I would be a writer. I called her 33 years later to tell her so.

To my *Divine Wisdom at Work*™ "Dream Team." Jeanne Sharbuno, my personal business coach for many years, led me through the sometimes arduous and often exhilarating writing process and then skillfully edited my manuscript as if it was her own. Scott Barnes, my computer consultant for many years, stepped up to build my website—fully anticipating the many ways it would inspire and support others on their Divine Wisdom journey. Garon Hart, my graphic designer, patiently worked with this first-time author to translate my vision of the book and make it real, inside and out.

Thank you to my dear friends and colleagues for their enthusiastic encouragement and thoughtful advice along the way, including Alison Ilg, Elizabeth Fairleigh, JoAnne Donner, Margo Geller, Loretta Vitale, Elizabeth Pagano, Phyllis Carrera, Greg Vetter, Kathy Bakon, Jayne Capetanakis, Tom Ellicott, Kim Arasin, Donna Huling, Stacey Mayo, Julie Squires, Laurie Farmer, Mandy Roth, Margaret Jones, Carol A. Hacker, Ken Futch and Connie R. Siewert.

With appreciation to fellow members of Toast of Cobb, a local chapter of Toastmasters International, for holding the vision of me as a dynamic, entertaining and inspiring speaker.

To my clients who inspired me over the years with their deep integrity and strong entrepreneurial spirit, including Don Whitney, Dan Smigrod, Eric Lindberg, Ken Menendez, Susan Pilgrim, David Geller, Millann Funk, Pat Adams, Mike Wittenstein and Mike Arasin.

To the inspiring entrepreneurs and business leaders I serendipitously met through the writing of this book who welcomed the opportunity to promote these principles that serve them so well in their own work. They include Jim Huling, Cindy LaFerle, Brian Johnson and Karen Drucker.

To my beloved minister for many years, Carole O'Connell, for reminding me of my innate wisdom through her Sunday messages and the way she lives her life. To my new ministers, Nancy and Bill Worth, for continuing to lovingly promote the powerful, positive, practical messages of Unity.

To our family beach house, which is both a tangible reminder of manifesting prosperity and a haven where most of the writing of this book flowed.

Most importantly, I thank my family. To our joyful dog, Honey, who has been my sweet companion during times of work and play. Thanks for reminding me that a brisk walk on a sunny day can bring a fresh perspective to any business dilemma.

To our magnificent children, Allyson and Connor Reyer, now 11 years old. May they pursue their own purpose and passion as they continue to connect with their Divine Wisdom.

And finally, to my devoted husband, Rick Reyer, for his wholehearted love, unabashed pride and genuine support of everything I do. Success is always certain with you by my side.

PREFACE

Our Greatest Fear

Our deepest fear is not that we are inadequate.
Our deepest fear is that we are powerful beyond measure.

It is our light, not our darkness, that most frightens us.
We ask ourselves, Who am I to be brilliant, gorgeous,
talented, fabulous?

Actually, who are you not to be?
You are a child of God.

Your playing small doesn't serve the world.
There's nothing enlightened about shrinking
so that other people won't feel insecure around you.

We are all meant to shine, as children do.
We were born to make manifest the glory of God that is
within us.

It's not just in some of us; it's in everyone.
And as we let our own light shine,
we subconsciously give other people permission to do the same.

As we're liberated from our own fear,
our presence automatically liberates others.

—Marianne Williamson from *A Return to Love*

INTRODUCTION

You are an Enlightened Entrepreneur

You hold a pencil in front of you and release it. It drops to the floor. That's the power of gravity.

You put a pot of water on the stovetop and turn it on. In a few minutes, the water begins to boil. That's the power of fire.

You throw away the files of three former small clients who weren't a good match for what you do. Then the phone rings with the prospect of a large client who appreciates what you have to offer. By clearing out the physical and emotional clutter, you make room for what most serves your highest good. That's the power of the universe abhorring a vacuum.

Setting intentions, affirming and visualizing success, embracing prosperity, giving thanks and all the other universal principles in *Divine Wisdom at Work*™ are ancient truths and powerful tools for today's business environment. They produce a competitive edge that sets you apart from most other entrepreneurs. They also turn work into play as you create, manage and grow your business with joy and ease.

◆

Policies are many.

Principles are few.

Policies will change.

Principles never do.

JOHN C. MAXWELL

◆

The good news is you were born with all this innate wisdom. Unfortunately, without the support and validation from others as you were growing up—and most likely a good dose of negative reinforcement—much of this wisdom has remained dormant. Think of this book as a "refresher course." As you rediscover each principle, you're sure to have many "aha!" moments.

As a business owner, personal business coach, marketing consultant and freelance business writer since 1988, I put these principles into action every day and share them with my clients and colleagues. As a board member at Unity North Atlanta Church for seven years, I was continually called on to integrate these universal principles with sound business practices to address the challenges and opportunities of our growing church. It is now one of the largest Unity churches in the world and a role model for other churches.

When I started sharing my "philosophy" with others who were curious, I recognized that these concepts didn't come naturally to most people. But once they began using them, they got results, whether it was more business or a more peaceful workplace. In fact, it was my own Life Purpose Statement (see principle two on how to write yours) that set the stage for this book:

Through support and by example,
I inspire others to follow their dreams and live joyfully on purpose.

In addition to helping you enhance your business, you'll also find that these principles will help transform your personal life, including achieving optimum health, attracting the right mate and friends, and being a better parent. Your example will inspire others to do the same.

In *Divine Wisdom at Work*,™ each of the ten principles builds on the next but can be taken in random order, depending on your specific interests or challenges.

I will introduce you to, or reacquaint you with, outstanding experts in the practice of practical spirituality. The anecdotes and advice from successful entrepreneurs, corporate executives and business consultants bring these principles to life and help you understand how to incorporate them in your own business. By experimenting with the suggested exercises, you will immediately put these principles into action to reap the rewards.

Now is the time to release fear and doubt and feel the pure exhilaration of being an enlightened entrepreneur through *Divine Wisdom at Work*.™ Enjoy the journey!

What is a New Thought Business Leader?

Tricia Molloy is known as a New Thought business leader. A thought leader is a recognized expert in one's field. A New Thought business leader is a recognized expert in the practice of practical spirituality in the workplace.

"New Thought is the great spiritual movement that came into being over one hundred years ago with the American Transcendentalists, including Emerson and Thoreau, with roots extending to Socrates and Plato," explains Reverend Mary Manin Morrissey in *Building Your Field of Dreams*. "New Thought is the fruiting of the flower found in all the great religions; it differs from more traditional teaching primarily in that it focuses on the message rather than the messenger. New Thought emphasizes increasing awareness in order to produce greater heath, better relationships and an abundance that leads to a deeply fulfilling life."

SUCCESS TIPS

*Getting the Most from **Divine Wisdom at Work**™*

If you're like most motivated, well-intentioned entrepreneurs, you read many business books each year. These books are filled with great ideas that energize and inspire you. However, without the support to execute and maintain them, you quickly return to business as usual. This time, it will be different.

Here are four strategies to put the *Divine Wisdom at Work*™ principles into practice:

1) Form a *Divine Wisdom at Work*™ business group. Invite other like-minded entrepreneurs to meet on a regular basis. Start with a planning session to decide how to proceed. You might meet once a month for breakfast at a restaurant or once a week after work at alternating offices. You can choose to focus on a particular principle for each meeting or let whatever challenges or opportunities the members currently face set the agenda. *Trust that you will be divinely guided.*

Always save room for acknowledging and celebrating the successes along the way. Consider ending each meeting with a bit of "Divine Homework" that will help establish new habits, like developing an affirmation around a business goal or writing consistently in your gratitude journal.

2) Introduce your team to *Divine Wisdom at Work*™ principles. Encourage your employees and perhaps key consultants and vendors to incorporate these principles into their daily practice. Recognize someone each month with public acknowledgement and a small reward, like a restaurant gift card.

3) Schedule a *Divine Wisdom at Work*™ coaching or consulting session or presentation. In select circumstances, I am available to coach and consult on these principles, as well as speak to employees and business associations. To find out more, go to www.divinewisdomatwork.com.

4) Share ideas with others and learn from them. Visit www.divinewisdomatwork.com to post your questions and share your successes. With your help, we can build a strong, growing community of enlightened entrepreneurs!

—**Tricia Molloy**

Tap into Divine Wisdom: Your Inner Guidance is Calling

Every moment of your life is infinitely creative and the universe is endlessly bountiful. Just put forth a clear enough request, and everything your heart desires must come to you.

MAHATMA GANDHI

Today you will hire a business partner. No need to worry about finding office space, budgeting for a salary or even placing an ad. This partner is already here but has been sadly underused and neglected. Your business partner is a powerful force with all the wisdom of the universe and always has your best interests at heart. It's your Higher Power or Higher Consciousness—the Divine Wisdom within you that you can access at any time for a wealth of information, ideas, support and guidance.

You don't have to know all the answers; you just need to know where to look. And often the place to look is inside.

There are many ways to tap into this inner guidance and co-create everything you desire. In this first chapter that begins your *Divine Wisdom at Work*™ journey, we will explore practicing meditation, trusting your intuition, looking for "God Winks," consulting with "the committee of sleep" and praying. You'll find the answers to many of your business and personal questions, including the ones you didn't know you had.

"We are not human beings on a spiritual journey. We are spiritual beings on a human journey," notes Stephen R. Covey, author of *The 7 Habits of Highly Effective People*. "I'm convinced that we can write and live our own scripts more than most people will acknowledge. I also know the price that must be paid. It's a real struggle to do it. It requires visualization and affirmation. It involves living a life of integrity, starting with making and keeping promises, until the whole human personality, the senses, the thinking, the feeling, and the intuition are ultimately integrated and harmonized."

"I believe there is a Power within each of us that can lovingly direct us to our perfect health, perfect relationships, perfect careers, and which can bring us prosperity of every kind," writes Louise Hay, a leader in the self-help movement and author of *The Power Is Within You* and the classic mind-body connection book *Heal Your Body*. "In order to have these things, we have to believe first that they are possible. Next, we must be willing to release the patterns in our lives that are creating conditions we say we do not want. We do this by going within and tapping the Inner Power that already knows what is best for us. If we are willing to turn our lives over to this greater Power within us, the Power that loves and sustains us, we can create more loving and prosperous lives."

> **Meditation is the tongue of the soul and the language of our spirit.**
>
> JEREMY TAYLOR

Meditation 101

It is said that praying is talking to God and meditating is listening to God. You might think that sitting still, going within and listening to Divine Wisdom would be fairly easy to do. For many of us, it can be one of the most challenging activities we will ever endeavor.

3

If you imagine someone wrapped in robes sitting cross-legged on a mountaintop, the process only gets more difficult. Even the word can be intimidating. I choose to say "checking in" instead. Whatever you call it or however you get there, you'll find that this ancient Eastern custom will help you relax, put things in perspective and gain remarkable insights.

You may choose to meditate first thing in the morning or before you go to sleep. You could set aside some time during your workday, making sure you are not interrupted. Hold your phone calls and try hanging on your office doorknob a hotel "Do Not Disturb" sign. Your colleagues will learn to respect this time and may even choose to follow your lead.

While you can consult many superb books and CDs to learn about meditation, like Jon Kabat-Zinn's *Wherever You Go, There You Are* and Jack Kornfield's *Meditation for Beginners*, I will share a few tips that have worked for me. First, remember there is no one right way to meditate. By experimenting, you will find the way that's right for you.

"The most important idea is that it's not as easy to open up to spiritual experience as we would like," advises James Redfield, author of *The Celestine*

> **The more often you go inside for answers, the sooner you will establish a rapport with the voice of your soul.**
>
> JEAN-MARIE HAMEL

Prophecy. "There are some psychological breakthroughs that need to happen. Learning how not to control others and how not to control our lives so intensely are two of those breakthroughs. We have to let go."

Let's Begin

Sit comfortably with your spine straight. Keep your hands facing palms upward on your legs, as a sign of receptivity. Think of them as small satellite dishes tuning into the universe. Pay special attention to your breath to clear your mind and connect with the infinite intelligence. Breathe fully from your diaphragm and experiment with different counts. Try breathing in for a count of three, holding for a count of four and breathing out for a count of six. Establish a rhythm so you can soon stop counting.

At the beginning of meditation, some people prefer using a mantra they say to themselves in rhythm with their breathing. Yours may be "All is well," "I am open to receive," "Thank you, Spirit" or "Om," which rhymes with "home." Om is said to be the sound of the creation of the universe and is considered the most powerful of all mantras. Sages claim that the vibration it produces—as you maintain the sound with your outward breath—puts you in touch with the wisdom of the universe. It slows down the breathing, calms the nervous system and gives your body's glands and organs a vibrational massage. Let's say it together: Ohhhhhmmmmmmmmmmm.....

Experiment with silence or soft instrumental music or nature sounds. You might picture the details of a relaxing setting like a meadow by a stream or a deserted tropical island. What do you see, feel, hear and smell? Hold a shell, pebble or other item to connect with this special place. Or you may choose to focus on the hypnotic flickering flame of a candle. Use whatever helps you enter a clear, calm state.

Stop judging your initial inability to get still. We all have constant chatter in our minds. Each time a thought pops into your head, acknowledge it and release it like a bubble that floats away. The time of stillness will increase as the thoughts decrease. I promise you that.

Before meditation, consider setting an intention, such as a more productive workplace, or posing a question like, "How can I attract ideal clients?" Recognize that meditation takes many forms. If it's too uncomfortable to sit still, try incorporating meditation in your walking regimen or yoga practice.

Keep your ego in check and refrain from trying to determine the outcome. "If you want to reach a state of bliss, then go beyond your ego and the internal dialogue," advises Deepak Chopra, M.D., renowned in the field of mind body medicine and author of *The Seven Spiritual Laws of Success*. "Make a decision to

◆

> What the world craves today is a more spiritual and less formal religion.
>
> J.D. ROCKEFELLER

◆

relinquish the need to control, the need to be approved, and the need to judge. Those are the three things the ego is doing all the time. It's very important to be aware of them every time they come up." Think of EGO as standing for "edging God out," so the next time you find your ego getting in the way, you can acknowledge and release it and welcome God in.

Be patient. Start small, promising yourself that you will meditate five minutes a day three days a week. Once you accomplish that, increase the time and days until you build up to 30 minutes a day perhaps twice a day every day. Above all, expect extraordinary ideas and solutions to come from meditating. It's one of the most powerful investments of time you can make for yourself and your business.

As the executive director of a nonprofit organization experiencing "growing pains," Tom Ellicott was under pressure to figure out a way to control costs, increase revenues and continue to enhance services. "I arrived at my office at seven one morning, determined to find a solution," recalls Ellicott, a former corporate sales manager. Instead of going straight for his desk and email, he walked across the room and sat down. He got quiet and began to meditate. "I asked God, 'What should I do about our financial problems?' I wasn't expecting to hear anything, but a small voice said, 'You don't have any financial problems.' I can not tell you how comforting that was for me. Just to hear those words gave me the faith to continue to work on the numbers in a positive way."

Go with Your Gut

Do you trust your intuition? The last time you found yourself in a situation that "felt" totally right or completely wrong, did you respect those feelings and respond accordingly? It's that first impression you have of a prospective client at a networking event. It's that small voice that tells you to delay your hiring decision until the candidate's final reference calls back. It's that figurative "red flag" that you see when the promises of an ambitious new printer seem too good to be true. It's what helps you capitalize on a time-sensitive opportunity where, if you were to wait for all the facts to come in, it would be too late.

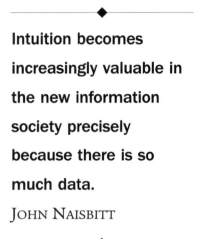

Intuition becomes increasingly valuable in the new information society precisely because there is so much data.

John Naisbitt

Tap into your sixth sense by simply asking. Let's say you are trying to decide whether to offer a new service, expand into a new market or end a frustrating client relationship. Ask yourself how you feel if you were to do it and monitor your physical reaction. Do a "gut check." Has your breath become shallow and are your muscles a little tighter? Or are you relaxed and loose? Now, repeat that observation as if you were to decide not to do it.

DIVINE

DIRECTIONS

Play with the concept of intuition. Try guessing at simple things like who might call you today or who you should call. The next time you are browsing a bookstore, ask Spirit to guide you and you may find yourself being drawn to just the right book on the shelf. (I do that a lot.) Follow your instincts to the right page as you surf the Internet in search of specific information or when casually flipping through a magazine. Give yourself permission to daydream and spend some time in nature every day. Journaling can also sharpen your intuition. Keep track of decisions you make based on your hunches or gut feelings and check the results. As your success rate increases, you will be more likely to trust your instincts.

Malcolm Gladwell, the author of *The Tipping Point* and *Blink*, is a proponent of rapid cognition—those instant conclusions we make every day. "When it comes to something like dating, we all readily admit to the importance of what happens in the first instant when two people meet," he says. "But we won't admit to the importance of what happens in the first two seconds when we talk about what happens when someone encounters a new idea, or when we interview someone for a job, or when a military general has to make a decision in the heat of battle."

Inspirational singer/songwriter Karen Drucker trusted her instincts when she was ready to reach the next level of her business. For about 20 years, this San Francisco-based artist performed at weddings, corporate events and New Thought churches. She was also a music director at three churches throughout her career. "I was ready to reach more people with my music," she says. "I just wasn't sure how to do it."

> When you were born, you cried and the world rejoiced. Live your life so that when you die, the world cries and you rejoice.
>
> CHEROKEE INDIAN SAYING

While browsing at a bookstore, she found *Inner Peace for Busy People* by Joan Borysenko, Ph.D. Or, as Drucker remembers, it found her. "The book seemed to throw itself off the shelf at me. I had never even heard of Joan but as I began to read through the book, I was amazed that so many of the words and phrases and messages were the same ones I use in my songs." A Harvard-trained psychologist and medical scientist, Dr. Borysenko brings science, medicine, psychology and spirituality together in the service of healing. Drucker visited Borysenko's website and saw that she was hosting a women's retreat in Arizona.

She called to see if they needed someone to perform music. The good news was that they did need someone to sing, play piano and lead the chanting and drumming, which was something Drucker loved to do. PBS was planning to videotape the event for a "Women of Wisdom and Power" television special. The bad news was they had nothing in their budget to pay someone, not even for travel expenses or for the piano rental.

"My business mind told me that it was ridiculous to even consider an offer like this," she recalls. "But my gut told me to go for it. I took the gig and it totally changed my life."

Drucker developed a professional and personal relationship with Borysenko. "We tour on a regular basis now and enjoy sharing our messages of empowerment. It's also fun to have a girlfriend to explore cities together. One of my songs, "Lighten Up," is referenced in her follow-up book, *Inner Peace for Busy Women*—on page 40. It cracks me up how one choice to trust my intuition could have such an impact." Drucker's songs, which range from the soft and sacred "Breathe" to the upbeat and sassy "I've Lost the Right to Sing the Blues," celebrate universal principles like prosperity consciousness, gratitude, forgiveness and listening to Divine Wisdom.

Through the United Church of Religious Science, Drucker learned: "Treat and move your feet." "We can meditate, pray, visualize and tap into our inner guidance all day long but then we must take action. It's a team effort. My business decisions are based on friendship, love and connection with Spirit. I use this as a model for everything I do."

God Winks

In *When God Winks*, author SQuire Rushnell (yes, the Q is capped) encourages us to pay attention to the synchronicities of life. "Think about it. If you were God and wanted to communicate with human beings without using a human voice, how would you do it? You'd perform little miracles, wouldn't you? You'd create little miracles, like coincidences, that cause people to say, 'What are the odds of this ever happening?' Those are God Winks."

> When you examine the lives of the most influential people who have ever walked among us, you discover one thread that winds through them all. They have been aligned first with their spiritual nature and only then with their physical selves.
>
> ALBERT EINSTEIN

One of my favorite "God Winks" came as I was briskly walking alone on the beach during a family vacation. I envisioned putting the final touches on my book and began to realize that for the longest time writing this book was more of a personal quest and now it had become a business venture. As I played with the idea of whether or not my little project could be profitable, I stopped and looked down at my feet to find a small, perfect sand dollar. We have never seen a sand dollar on this beach, ever.

God winked to remind me to think abundantly. The sand dollar, which I carefully packed away for my trip back home and then placed in a frame, serves me well as I continue my journey as a successful, prosperous author. Think about the "God Winks" you've had, perhaps when you've felt doubt or fear or when you faced a crossroads in your business. Keep looking for those "God Winks."

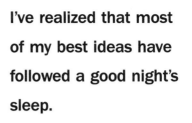

I've realized that most of my best ideas have followed a good night's sleep.

THOMAS EDISON

To Sleep, Perchance to Dream

Pulitzer and Nobel Prize-winning novelist John Steinbeck achieved worldwide recognition for his keen observations and powerful descriptions of the human condition. The author of *The Grapes of Wrath* once said, "It is a common experience that a problem difficult at night is resolved in the morning after the committee of sleep has worked on it." Many prominent artists like Surrealist painter Salvador Dali and musician Paul McCartney have attributed the source of their creations to dreams. So did Albert Einstein.

According to the International Association for the Study of Dreams, a nonprofit organization dedicated to investigating this phenomenon, dreams are useful in learning more about the dreamer's feelings, thoughts, behavior, motives and values. Dreams can help solve problems and enhance your creativity.

Are you trying to write a compelling sales letter, choose new software or effectively reward your top producers? Why don't you sleep on it? Everyone dreams but the details of our dreams often drift away soon after we awake. Keep paper and a pen on your night table. You might use a flashlight or find a pen with a tip that lights up. If you wake in the middle of the night, you want a light bright enough to see but soft enough not to wake you completely.

Dreams are often most profound when they seem the most crazy.

SIGMUND FREUD

Are you ready to summon "the committee of sleep"? Start by clearing your mind of distractions. Refrain from watching television or reading that evening. Take a moment to decide what problem you want to solve and write it down. Visualize yourself dreaming about the problem. You may even choose to add some symbolic items to your night table. Or you could draw the result, like a group of happy clients. When you write down your dreams, don't get discouraged if they don't quite make sense. Keep a dream diary. It may take time before that "light bulb" goes off and you understand the connection between the images or scenarios and your solution.

Monique A. Dearth started her own human resources consulting firm after an eight-year career at General Electric (GE). "I left GE knowing I would return to do some contract work for them, and it really began as a joke that I would name my company MAD HR," she says. "My initials are MAD and I always sign my emails MAD, which is in direct contrast to my upbeat personality." Then, business began to grow and expand outside of GE. She started doing work for The Home Depot and other companies and got more than a few odd looks when she told people she was with MAD HR. "It was time to bring some other people on to complete all the work. I knew the timing was right to re-brand MAD HR with a new name, logo and website."

After agonizing for months over what to call her company, she vividly recalls going to bed one Friday night in October 2002 and asking God for some guidance. "I thoroughly believe that we can ask questions and receive answers through our spirituality and our subconscious mind. I recall smiling that night as I asked my question because, in the scheme of things in the world, this was not what you would call 'a burning question.'"

That night, she dreamed she was out for a casual late night walk through a neighborhood and came across people running down the streets and fires burning. "It was not chaotic or frightening at all. It just was what it was. I walked up to a police officer and asked what was going on and he said something to the effect of, 'someone incited a riot.' I said, 'Okay,' and kept on strolling. That was the end of it. Nothing complex, nothing monumental. But, when I awoke the next morning it was as clear as day and I knew I had been given the name of my company, Incite Strategies."

Prayer is moving into a personal relationship with Divine Intelligence.

GARY ZUKAV

The dictionary defines incite as: to move to action, stir up, spur on, encourage, impel, stimulate, motivate. Dearth says, "Through our training, coaching, assessments and other consulting services, I like to think we incite our clients—encouraging, motivating and impelling them towards becoming better leaders."

The Power of Prayer

I left this daunting subject until last because prayer is such a sacred, personal practice, often steeped in childhood religious traditions. Who am I to tell you how to do it? This is what I know to be true for me. When I pray for wisdom and guidance regarding my business, it might be for the right and perfect business associate or to determine how to grow more profitably. Decide what you will pray for.

First, recognize that there is only one power in the universe and that is God. Next, recognize that this loving God is within you, guiding you at all times. State your desire as a clear affirmation, such as "I attract clients who appreciate and support me." (See principle nine on affirmations.) Engage the emotions you would feel if your prayer was already answered. Always give thanks "for this or something better" and detach from the final outcome since Spirit may have something far more glorious for you than you could ever imagine.

> **Sometimes the answer to prayer is not that it changes life, but that it changes you.**
>
> JAMES DILLETT FREEMAN

The most powerful prayer is sometimes simply, "Help me, God." God already knows the rest. Don't limit your prayers to just requests. "You pray in your distress and in your need," wrote poet and philosopher Kahlil Gibran. "Would that you might also pray in the fullness of your joy and in your days of abundance."

Tyson Foods, the world's largest producer of meat and a faith-friendly company, employs more than 114,000 people at over 300 facilities around the world. In 1999, CEO and Chairman John Tyson, the grandson of the founder of the company, established a proactive employee assistance program to address the spiritual needs of its workers. Many of their production facilities feature chaplains who counsel and pray with employees at their request. "The chaplains administer by wandering around—the hallways, breakrooms, offices—informally making themselves available," says Alan Tyson, director of chaplain services and no relation to John Tyson.

They respond at times of crisis, like a death or serious illness. They also help employees deal with workplace conflicts and marital, health and financial problems. "Whatever may be troubling them, our employees know they can talk to and pray with a neutral, caring person," he says. "We've seen an increase in team member morale and a drop in turnover. Our human resources people love it because they are not usually trained to handle the issues that the chaplains do."

The chaplains are part-time team members affiliated with nearby places of worship. In addition to supplementing their income, this program provides other benefits to them. "Working with our people at Tyson energizes the chaplains and helps them appreciate the challenges their own congregation faces during the week," says Tyson, who expects this program to continue to grow as the company grows.

In her book, *Hiring the Heavens: A Practical Guide to Developing Working Relationships with the Spirits of Creation*, Jean Slatter reminds us to never underestimate the power of the spoken word. "Your request will hold more conviction if you say it out loud," she says. "Our minds are full of endless chatter. Anyone tuning in would find it difficult to know when we really mean something and when it's just a lot of jumbled rambling."

Slatter continues, "Using our voice helps us get our own attention and focus on what we really want. I find that when I speak out loud, my sentences are far more coherent. I imagine a presence, an intelligent energy listening as I explain my request. I don't picture this energy as a person, or give it a personal name, but you might like to try that. Do whatever works best for you! Don't waste even a minute feeling embarrassed. The universe feels nothing but delight in being involved with every endeavor of your life, and it enthusiastically waits to hear your thoughts and ideas."

PRINCIPLE 1
TAP INTO DIVINE WISDOM:
YOUR INNER GUIDANCE IS CALLING

◆ Just like your cell phone keeps you in touch with the office and home while you're away, the five strategies in chapter one keep you in touch with your Divine Wisdom.

◆ Meditation helps you get still and quiet so you can hear the small voice inside.

◆ Intuition is relying on your gut instincts instead of second-guessing yourself and letting fear get in the way.

◆ Use dreams to intentionally solve problems and get creative.

◆ "God Winks," meaningful coincidences or synchronicities, can be Divine Signs, especially at times of doubt or fear or when you face a crossroads in your business.

◆ Prayer, both at times of need and in gratitude, keeps you connected.

Define Your Life Purpose: Setting Intentions

I've come to believe that each of us has a personal calling that's as unique as a fingerprint—and that the best way to succeed is to discover what you love and then find a way to offer it to others in the form of service, working hard, and also allowing the energy of the universe to lead you.

OPRAH WINFREY

Why are you here and how does your work support that? Some believe that, before we are born, we have agreed to accomplish something important while we are on this earth. That proclamation shows up as our life purpose. The best life purposes are twofold: a personal quest and one that benefits others, which might be family members, coworkers, your community or even the world. It is what we are most passionate about, what excites and propels us, what comes most naturally to us. It's often a source of high joy and what we would do even if we weren't paid for it. It is our sacred service to others and ourselves. Once you define your life purpose, you will begin to set intentions that align with it.

"The meaning of life is creative love," writes Tom Morris, Ph.D., contemporary philosopher and author of *If Aristotle Ran General Motors*. "Not love as an inner feeling, as a private sentimental emotion, but love as a dynamic power moving out into the world and doing something original. In business and in life, it means the creative building of new structures, new relationships and new solutions. New possibilities for our world that are rooted in love, concern for the dignity and integrity and value of others in this life."

One Man's Life Purpose

From as far back as he can remember, Don Whitney knew his life purpose was to help children who couldn't help themselves. He was one of seven children who had his basic needs met and assumed everyone else did too. Then, when he was 12, a television infomercial showing destitute children in a faraway country forever changed his life. "I remember feeling so thankful and wondered why these children didn't have enough food or a home or a mom and dad to take care of them," he recalls. "I knew of a loving God who cares for all children and it was clear to me that it was my role to help God do that."

> When we do what we are meant to do, money comes to us, doors open for us, we feel useful, and the work we do feels like play to us.
>
> JULIA CAMERON

Although Whitney didn't receive an allowance, he worked at the local pizza parlor for 75 cents an hour and delivered newspapers. At 13, he sponsored his first child, a six-year-old girl from Indonesia. "I began by sending $12 a month and I felt I could make a difference." He continued to sponsor more children over the years. He and his wife, Cathy, and their twin sons now sponsor and support 21 children from organizations all over the world. They often visit these children to make a personal connection and to assure that the organizations are fulfilling their promise.

In 1980, when Whitney was just 22, he established Corporate Sports Unlimited, a team building and special events planning company. In addition to producing more than 250 events a year worldwide, the company builds and manages executive health clubs. Longtime clients include IBM and The Coca-Cola Company. Corporate Sports was named the Atlanta Chamber of Commerce's "Small Business of the Year" and, out of more than 100 competitors, was the runner up in the business division for Ernst & Young's Entrepreneur of the Year for Georgia, Alabama and Tennessee.

> The biggest mistake that people make in life is not trying to make a living at doing what they most enjoy.
>
> MALCOLM FORBES

As the president of The U.S. 10K Classic, an annual, international road racing event he founded in 1994, Whitney donates all proceeds to a variety of children's charities. In its first decade, this event has raised more than $900,000 for such organizations as the Boys & Girls Clubs of America, Prevent Child Abuse Georgia and several homeless ministries.

But this wasn't enough. Whitney had established strong corporate contacts through his business and the race. He saw how the executives of Publix Super Markets, BellSouth and other corporate giants were also seeking more innovative and lasting ways to give back. That vision led to creating the World Children's Center, a planned community for approximately 500 homeless, orphaned and neglected children from Georgia, the United States and the world. More than 75 sponsors support this vision.

"When my time is done on this earth, I will not be measured by what I've taken, but by what I've given back," he says. "I am driven to use what He blessed me with to advance His love for all of us. And, I am blessed that so many successful entrepreneurs and business executives share this quest with me."

Whitney offers this advice to entrepreneurs who want to promote their life purpose through their work. "First, create a balanced life that encompasses faith, family, friends, work and taking care of yourself. I have seen too many people who focus solely on being successful at work and making money while everything around them crumbles. It's a hollow victory. Despite our hectic schedules, my wife and I try to honor a weekly date night and I coach my sons' baseball team," he says. "Surround yourself with positive people on the same path for the support you'll need to accomplish extraordinary things. Start small and keep building. Finally, trust that God is with you every step of the way."

> Everything—a horse, a vine—is created for some duty...For what task, then, were you yourself created? A man's true delight is to do the things he was made for.
>
> MARCUS AURELIUS

Raising the World's Consciousness
Through the Internet

Brian Johnson is an Internet entrepreneur who follows his purpose and passion. He graduated magna cum laude with Phi Beta Kappa honors from the University of California, Los Angeles, where he studied psychology and business. A short stint as a consultant at Arthur Andersen, followed by a semester at Boalt Law School at the University of California, Berkeley, showed him a few things he wasn't supposed to do.

"Working at Arthur Andersen and the prospects of becoming an attorney looked good but it never felt right," he says. "Although I wasn't sure exactly what my purpose was, I felt a deeper calling and I had a gnawing, unsettled feeling that I wasn't on the right path. So, I dropped out of law school and took a plunge into the unknown."

In 1998, shortly after leaving law school, he was coaching a boys' baseball team and envisioned how the Internet could enhance a family's experience with sports. He could see that in a matter of time every team and league around the world would be using the Internet for everything from schedules and standings to pictures of the kids that Grandma and Grandpa would check out if they couldn't make the game.

Johnson and his partner cracked open their piggy banks and invested $5,000 each to create www.eteamz.com, an online team sports community where amateur teams could easily set up websites. After winning the UCLA business plan competition and raising several million dollars, eteamz became the world's largest amateur sports website and the official website for Little League Baseball.® They sold it in 2000 for more than $13 million in stock and cash. It currently serves more than two million teams in over 120 countries.

After selling that business at 26, Johnson embarked on a mission to discover what he's here to do. During this time, he traveled to the Middle East and parts of Central and Western Europe, where he studied Socrates in Athens, Rumi in Turkey, Jesus in Jerusalem and Marcus Aurelius in the Danube of Hungary. He read voraciously, studying a range of philosophies and religions, as well as creative learning techniques, leadership, nutrition and exercise science. In the process, he discovered that he was passionate about understanding the universal truths of optimal living and inspiring and empowering others to do the same. So, he created an inspiring website called www.thinkarete.com. Ancient Greek philosophers like Socrates, Plato and Aristotle taught that the meaning of life was happiness and that the way to achieve happiness was to live with areté—which is the process of self-actualization and striving to reach your highest potential. His mission for the website is to distill the universal truths of the world's great philosophers, mystics and psychologists and share their wisdom to inspire people to think and to create their own philosophy of life.

"Many people who consider going into business for themselves are looking for 'the next big thing' on which to capitalize," he says. "Instead, I believe we should look within and identify what our gifts are and how we can share them with the world." By studying with Martin Seligman, Ph.D., the author of *Authentic Happiness*, and taking a VIA (Values in Action Institute) Signature Strength test through www.authentichappiness.org, Johnson confirmed a few things about his gifts. "These are my strengths: Creativity, hope and optimism—which makes sense because I'm always looking for new ways to do things and I have no doubt that we can all achieve our dreams. Kindness

> Man's ideal state is realized when he has fulfilled the purpose for which he is born. And what is it that reason demands of him? Something very easy—that he live in accordance with his own nature.
>
> SENECA

and generosity—I get a lot out of giving to others. Wisdom—which is why I love to offer perspective and give advice, whether it's my own guidance or something I read by a famous psychologist or spiritual teacher. Courage—which allows me to take risks. And plenty of energy—which shows up in my extreme and often contagious enthusiasm!"

Armed with self awareness, Johnson is now the philosopher and CEO of Zaadz, Inc. The company is integrating spirituality, capitalism and technology to help create businesses that change the world. "Zaadz, at www.zaadz.com, is evolving into an online community of seekers and enlightened entrepreneurs who get to profitably share their message with the broadest audience possible," he says. "This website will have a direct and significant impact on raising the overall consciousness of our world." And so it is.

How important is it to pursue our life purpose through our work? Ask Laurence G. Boldt, author of the groundbreaking *Zen and the Art of Making a Living* and *How to Find the Work You Love.* "We cannot read the writings of Aristotle, the sayings of Confucius, or the teachings of the Buddha, the Bible, Koran, or Bhagavad-Gita without sooner or later encountering a theory of vocational choice," he writes. "The world's great spiritual and philosophical traditions have long recognized the central role that vocational choice plays in the total health and happiness of the individual and in the vitality and character of a culture."

> A musician must make music, an artist must paint, a poet must write, if he is to be ultimately at peace with himself.
>
> ABRAHAM MASLOW

Defining Your Life Purpose

If the mere idea of defining your life purpose produces the same anxiety you felt in college when you were asked to choose a major, you're not alone. It sounds so important and so final. Over the years, though, many of us have diverted from what we once expected to be our life work. The same is true with a life purpose. The life purpose you choose now may evolve and even metamorphose into something different and greater and just as perfect for who you are at that time.

Like a business's Mission Statement, a Life Purpose Statement helps define and guide us. When faced with tough decisions, it is what we consult to determine alignment with our most sacred values and motivations. In 1997, a friend and personal coach recommended that I write down my life purpose and post it prominently in my office. I wasn't even sure what a life purpose was. Looking back, I think it was her way of removing the mystery from the process. She made me believe that she assumed I already had formulated one.

What I knew to be true was that I have always naturally shared advice and my own experiences with others. Often when I succeeded at something, whether it was building a business or overcoming infertility, I would reflect on how I could help others do the same. After a process and a series of edits, I decided on this: *Through support and by example, I inspire others to follow their dreams and live joyfully on purpose.* This framed Life Purpose Statement sits atop my office credenza behind my desk. I think of it often, especially when I am coaching and mentoring others and pursuing my own joy through work. This statement is what guided me to write the book you are holding right now.

You may already intuitively know your life purpose and just need to wordsmith it until

> **To begin to think with purpose is to enter the ranks of those strong ones who only recognize failure as one of the pathways to attainment.**
>
> James Allen

it sounds right. However, if you need help defining yours, here's an exercise. According to José Stevens, Ph.D., the author of *The Power Path: The Shaman's Way to Success in Business and Life*, there are nine basic needs which motivate us. These are:

1) security (control)
2) expansion (growth)
3) acceptance (approval)
4) adventure (risk taking)
5) power (confidence)
6) communion (organizing groups)
7) freedom (independence)
8) expression (creativity)
9) exchange (sharing ideas and advice)

I recommend these six steps to formulate your Life Purpose Statement.

1) Choose the three motivators that resonate most with you and write them on the top of a piece of paper.

2) Take ten minutes to tap into your stream of consciousness by free writing about why those three are most important. Share the feelings they bring out in you and any personal anecdotes that illustrate them. Resist editing or pausing or questioning what you've written. When you are done, underline what you consider to be the five most significant messages and transfer those to a separate page.

3) Now consider what you value most, personally and professionally, such as honesty, harmony, family and financial independence. Make a list of all you can think of and then circle the ten key values.

4) Make a list of your strengths or natural gifts, like compassion and a sense of humor. Circle the top five.

5) Review your top three motivators, five messages from the free-writing exercise, ten key values and your five gifts.

6) When you're ready, begin to formulate your Life Purpose Statement. Live with it, play with it, fine tune it and, when it feels right, print it out and display it. Treat it with reverence for it will serve you in many ways.

Setting Intentions

An intention is the broad, bright light that leads the way for the more specific goals you set. It is the sacred promise made between your soul and the universe to take responsibility and assure the quality of what you will manifest. As it relates to your life purpose, your intentions for your business might include clear communications, complete integrity with customers and employees, and a fun, creative work environment. From there, you develop the goals that relate to each one.

> Intent is to humans what software is to a computer. When installed into your psyche, intent gives you access to new capabilities, which opens up new realities.
>
> Debbie Ford

DIVINE DIRECTIONS

Plan your day. You may also set an intention each morning about the kind of day you want to have. It might be high energy and productive or quiet and contemplative. As your day progresses, you will seek to connect with people and situations to support that intention. When your day begins to veer from the intention you set, you can correct the course and continue on your way.

One of the intentions that came from my Life Purpose Statement is: *Embrace joy*. The goals that followed this intention include:

✔ Take the time to play every day.

✔ Only work with clients I enjoy and respect.

✔ Surround myself with positive, happy people.

Consider this intention. "I have one life and one chance to make it count for something," said Jimmy Carter, the 39th president of the United States and founder of The Carter Center. "I'm free to choose what that something is, and the something I've chosen is my faith. Now, my faith goes beyond theology and religion and requires considerable work and effort. My faith demands—this is not optional—my faith demands that I do whatever I can, wherever I am, whenever I can, for as long as I can with whatever I have to try to make a difference." In 2002, Carter received the Nobel Peace Prize "for his decades of untiring effort to find peaceful solutions to international conflicts, to advance democracy and human rights, and to promote economic and social development."

When Wendy Y. Bailey of Brilliance in Action™ sets her intentions, she employs a combination of free writing, questions and deliberate visioning. "I allow my subconscious to lead me, without judging or editing what I write," says this personal and business coach for entrepreneurs. "I tend to write phrases, thoughts and feelings about my goals and ask questions like, "What does my life look like?' and 'What am I accomplishing?' as if these goals were already real." Bailey says this process is comfortable and fluid, not structured or rigid. "I trust that I don't have to control it, that the details will work themselves out."

That's what she did when she needed a team to help support her growing business. "I was tired of being the do-it-yourself girl," she says. "At the time, I had one virtual assistant and I knew, even with her, I needed more assistants—each with their own unique talents. Once I set my intentions and envisioned these assistants working and interacting with me, I quickly attracted the second one to me. I found the third because I had developed a very specific list of skill sets which drove my search." She didn't let financial concerns get in the way. "I knew once I had my team in place, the work would flow. My practice is very full now and I have a waiting list of clients."

Bailey uses this process with her clients. "Business owners come to me to help them see what's already there, the tremendous potential within them. When they picture a future ideal life and treat it like it's the present moment, they can begin to take the steps to get there."

When your intentions are set, you claim it to be true and you use tools like goal setting and affirmations to put the wheels in motion. The pieces to realizing these intentions will fall into place. Coincidences begin to occur. A helpful colleague calls you or an article or book appears on a specific topic you've been pondering. As with many of these universal principles, there is a scientific basis to this phenomenon. It's called your Reticular Activating System (RAS). Since your brain is bombarded by thousands of messages every second from all of your senses, this system acts as a filter to decide which ones get through. You can program your RAS by setting your intentions and accompanying goals. Create a process to measure where you are and where you want to be. Begin talking about this to others. The more you focus on these intentions, the more your RAS will help you realize them. Every principle and practice in this book will serve to support the intentions you set.

> Knowing others is intelligence; knowing yourself is true wisdom. Mastering others is strength; mastering yourself is true power.
>
> LAO TSU

Divine Aha's

PRINCIPLE 2
DEFINE YOUR LIFE PURPOSE: SETTING INTENTIONS

◆ Your life purpose may be twofold: a personal quest and one that benefits others.

◆ It is a source of high joy and a sacred service to others and yourself.

◆ To define your life purpose, you must first define your motivations, values and gifts.

◆ Once you have a written Life Purpose Statement, set intentions that support and reflect it.

◆ Make your life purpose your life's work.

Embrace Prosperity: You Deserve Unlimited Abundance

Money is congealed energy and
releasing it releases life's possibilities.

JOSEPH CAMPBELL

We all grew up with some forms of limiting beliefs based on our experiences and role models. You may believe that you are not smart enough or as creative as someone else because of something that happened in the past or simply a passing comment. Whatever those beliefs are, they stuck with you and you identify with them.

One of the most common limiting beliefs revolves around prosperity. You may not think you are worthy of abundance or you may believe that rich people lack integrity, are workaholics or are just much better or luckier than you. Or you may be irresponsible with money—spending more than you earn—and in a constant state of debt and fear. The truth is that absolute abundance is our birthright. Let me repeat that. Absolute abundance is our birthright.

"It is not on a whim that the founders of our country chose to have inscribed on every dollar bill the statement 'In God We Trust,'" surmises Arnold Patent in *Money & Beyond*. "They understood that our relationship with money derives from our relationship with God, and that if we did not trust in God, our Oneness, our relationship with money would reflect that lack of trust."

> ◆
>
> **When I chased after money, I never had enough. When I got my life on purpose and focused on giving of myself and everything that arrived in my life, then I was prosperous.**
>
> Dr. Wayne Dyer
>
> ◆

What does Money Mean to You?

Money is the last great taboo in society, less discussed than politics, religion and even sex. For some, money means freedom and security. For others, it's stifling responsibility and a way to keep score. American humorist Will Rogers said, "Too many people spend money they haven't earned to buy things they don't want to impress people they don't like."

> **Your financial blueprint consists of a combination of your thoughts, feelings, and actions in the arena of money.**
>
> T. HARV EKER

Abundance is much more than material possessions and the size of your bank account. It is health and energy, joyful relationships, and living each day with grace and ease. It is a clear knowing that there is no lack.

Things come to us by right of consciousness, not by chance. There is a spiritual law of giving and receiving. As we manage our money well and allow it to move freely and circulate, more money comes to us. Money is a tangible form of God energy.

In the classic prosperity book, *The Energy of Money*, author Maria Nemeth, Ph.D., explains that our relationship to money is reflected in all other areas of our life. It can be a perfect focal point for working out life's important lessons. "Successful people know how energy works," she writes. "They know how to focus the various kinds of energy—money, time, physical vitality, creativity, among others—to convert their ideas, dreams, and visions into reality. And they know how to do this with ease."

In *The 9 Steps to Financial Freedom: Practical & Spiritual Steps So You Can Stop Worrying*, Certified Financial Planner Professional,® columnist and talk show host Suze Orman said she learned about the dharma or "right actions" of money in a course on Eastern spiritual traditions. "Beyond a shadow of a doubt, I know the following principle is true: We experience prosperity, true financial freedom, when our actions with respect to money are dharmic, or righteous, actions—that is, actions of generosity, actions of offering."

> When you give consistently to God's work, you open the way to receive consistently.
>
> CATHERINE PONDER

Find a worthy recipient—like the place you are spiritually fed—and commit to consistently support it. The traditional rule is tithing 10 percent of your income. *The One Minute Manager* author, Ken Blanchard, Ph.D., understands how this works. "I absolutely believe in the power of tithing and giving back. My own experience about all the blessings I've had in my life is that the more I give away, the more that comes back. That is the way life works, and that is the way energy works."

DIVINE DIRECTIONS

Examine how you handle money, literally as well as figuratively. Suze Orman advises that we start by taking a look at our wallets. Are your bills neatly stacked in order of denominations, all facing the same way? Or are they crumbled and stuffed in or scattered in your bag or various pockets? This one simple exercise reveals so much about our level of respect and appreciation for money.

Are you spending more than you earn and indebted to high-interest loans and credit cards? Do you know your credit score? Are you prepared to capitalize on new opportunities by having a line of credit? When you make business purchases—from office furniture and supplies to technology—do you research your options and shop around? Do your basic business tools, such as your writing instruments and briefcase, reflect quality? Are you paying the best rates for your phone service? Do you use software to effortlessly track income and expenses? Are you sufficiently insured? Do you understand your investments and tax-saving strategies?

When it comes to money, it's more than what you bring in. It's also what you keep and how you choose to use it. Set an intention to gain control of your finances by tackling at least one of these questions each month, starting with the one that makes you squirm the most. Think of other financial issues that have not been addressed and add those to the list.

When you handle money well, you are empowered by knowing what you have and deciding where it will go.

Affirm Abundance

Prosperity affirmations are a good way to remind you of what is true. On the inside cover of my calendar, I have this one: "I attract high-quality, interesting, prosperous clients who are easy to work with, greatly appreciate my services, happily pay me what I'm worth and enthusiastically refer me to others. I work as many hours as I like and consistently make $8,000 or more a month." (The amount varies from year to year.) On the inside of my checkbook cover are the words: "I have more than enough money for a long and joyful life." And, printed on the check itself is: "God is my source."

> **It's a kind of spiritual snobbery that makes people think they can be happy without money.**
>
> ALBERT CAMUS

Lauriann Davies, of Leave it to Lauri, is a professional home-office organizer. She is passionate about helping clients find balance and harmony in their lives by showing them how to de-clutter and reorganize what is most important to them. It's a job she would almost do for free, but she knows the true value of her talent and was ready to increase her income. Lauriann tapped into the power of affirmations and added a dose of Feng Shui, the art of placement, to make it happen. (See more about Feng Shui in principle five.)

"I wrote on my business card, 'My business is prosperous and profitable,' placed it in a red envelope and put the envelope in the wealth corner of my home," she says. The very next week, her revenues increased by 50 percent and have maintained that level for the last few months. "I began to attract new clients through my website and reconnected with old ones. I also chose to hold onto all my checks I collected during the week and made one weekly deposit, as if I were depositing a weekly paycheck. That helped remind me that my weekly pay as an entrepreneur was much higher than when I worked for someone else."

> **We all have the extraordinary coded within us, waiting to be released.**
> JEAN HOUSTON

Consider this advice from Eric Butterworth, a Unity minister and author of *Spiritual Economics*. "Make a commitment to get yourself and keep yourself in the positive stream of life. Refuse to indulge in casual conversation about the bad economy, the high cost of living, or about anything you really do not want to say yes to. Eliminate such thoughts as 'I can't,' 'I'm afraid,' and 'There is not enough' from your consciousness. Talk only about the things you want to see live and grow. Keep your thoughts centered in the ideas of abundance, self-sufficiency, and well-being. And occasionally give yourself a consciousness boost by affirming something like: God is my instant, constant and abundant source of supply."

How can you remind yourself that you deserve and attract abundance of all kinds into your life? Consider what you say to others and yourself. Do you plan for high revenue, with the prospect of falling a little short but still ahead of where you may have been? Or do you keep your revenue goals "realistic" and "doable" so you can guarantee that you will reach them? The more you stretch your concept of what you can achieve, the closer you'll get to that ultimate goal. Surround yourself with people who "think big" and have already achieved many of your dreams.

> ◆
>
> **The greater danger for most of us lies not in setting our aim too high and falling short; but in setting our aim too low and achieving the mark.**
>
> MICHELANGELO
>
> ◆

"Both abundance and lack exist simultaneously in our lives, as parallel realities," writes Sarah Ban Breathnach, author of *Simple Abundance*. "It is always our conscious choice which secret garden we will tend. When we choose not to focus on what is missing from our lives but are grateful for the abundance that's present—love, health, family, friends, work, the joys of nature and personal pursuits that bring us pleasure—the wasteland of illusion falls away and we experience Heaven on earth."

Divine Aha's

PRINCIPLE 3
EMBRACE PROSPERITY:
YOU DESERVE UNLIMITED ABUNDANCE

- Absolute abundance is your birthright.

- When you truly believe you deserve prosperity—professionally and personally—you will begin to attract it.

- Money is tangible God energy that needs to be circulated to thrive.

- Prosperity affirmations can help increase your business's profits.

Clean Out the Clutter: The Universe Will Fill the Vacuum

We do not keep the outward form of order,

where there is deep disorder in the mind.

WILLIAM SHAKESPEARE

Clutter is everywhere. The physical clutter of paperwork, mail and reading materials on our desk and in our files seems to multiply on a regular basis. The electronic clutter of email and the proliferation of news and information from the Internet and a multitude of media outlets can be overwhelming and paralyzing. Then there's the emotional clutter of unfulfilled commitments, difficult clients, deals that got away, self-defeating thoughts and the "what ifs" that never seem to materialize.

Clutter distracts and confuses us and drains our energy—physically, mentally, emotionally and spiritually. Cleaning out the clutter on all levels allows the universe to detect a vacuum and fill it with our best intentions. Yes, the universe abhors a vacuum.

◆

Ninety-nine percent of the things you worry about never happen anyway.

JAMES MOLLOY

◆

When you identify and eliminate clutter, you can focus on what's most important and attract it into your business.

"Never again clutter your days or nights with so many menial and unimportant things that you have no time to accept a real challenge when it comes along," advises Og Mandino, author of *The Greatest Salesman in the World*. "This applies to play as well as work. A day merely survived is no cause for celebration. You are not here to fritter away your precious hours when you have the ability to accomplish so much by making a slight change in your routine. No more busy work. No more hiding from success. Leave time, leave space, to grow. Now. Now! Not tomorrow!"

I invite you to participate in a little experiment. Go to your drawer of old client files that you have kept "just in case" they reappear. Lay each file on the floor in front of you in two piles: the ones of clients you enjoyed working with and the ones you didn't. Throw away the second pile and clean up and organize the first. Then set an intention to attract a certain amount of new and former ideal clients. Write it down and watch what happens.

> A high-quality life has a lot more to do with what you remove from your life than what you add to it. Our lives change dramatically when we start letting go.
>
> CHERYL RICHARDSON

Chances are that some of the clients you affirmed were worthy of your services will resurface, especially if you check in with them. And new opportunities will manifest. If you hear from the clients whose files you purged, it will be easy to let them know they would be better served by someone else.

Clarity Begins at Home

Organizational and time management expert Joe Cirillo, author of *It's Your Time*, says we need to start with clearing the clutter at home before we can do it at work. He has been a business owner for more than thirty years.

"First, you must accept the fact that you are disorganized and you have way too much stuff," he says. "Once you are aware of this, you can start making changes that will greatly improve the quality of your life and your productivity." Cirillo recommends cleaning out the extra clothes in your closets, food in your pantry and freezer, and unnecessary credit cards and other junk in your bag or briefcase. Next, look at your bathroom countertops and closets, and the inside of your car. Organizing what's left is much easier when the garbage is gone.

Research shows you'll gain about two hours a day when you go from cluttered to clean. "By focusing on all you will achieve from living and working in a tidy environment," he says, "you will muster the motivation to get it done and keep it that way."

Value Your Time

The author of *Take Your Soul to Work*, Tanis Helliwell, recommends that we re-establish the balance between quality and quantity and between kairos and chronos time. "Chronos is clock time—doing time—and by utilizing it we can create in the material world," she says. "If we don't have a good grip on chronos time, we miss planes, are late for appointments and generally make a nuisance of ourselves. Kairos time—being time—is that of the eternal moment when we enter into a rhythm with the divine life force. It cannot be contained by our physical sense of reality and often expands or diminishes when it enters chronos time."

It starts with awareness and a commitment to set priorities. "We must be ruthless in determining what is important and say 'no' to distractions, low-priority items and quantity of experiences that keep us from states of peace that are found in a more leisurely life," she says. "This could be taking only one trip to the grocery store instead of four, meaning we have to plan better for what we'll be needing for the entire week. It could be restricting our use of television because its hypnotic, mind-numbing vibration can rob us of energy and consciousness. At work, it could mean doing top-priority items that have the greatest chances of positively impacting our world, such as market plans, product development, following up with clients, rather than doing the easy things that make little difference to achieving important

> **Until you value yourself, you will not value your time. Until you value your time, you will not do anything with it.**
>
> M. SCOTT PECK

goals, such as paying our bills daily, continually tidying the office or redoing the filing system. Yes, of course, these are necessary, but they must be offset by the amount of time we spend in doing high-priority items."

Helliwell says we can learn to work in "magical time," where chronos and kairos meet and extend the quality and quantity of time. "This might seem unlikely, but all of us have had experiences where time seemed to stop and we were able to accomplish an apparently impossible amount of work."

Terminate Your Tolerations

So, how do you eliminate those things that bug you, distract you and rob you of precious time but you've grown to tolerate? Business and personal coach Jeanne Sharbuno, the author of *52 Ways to Live Success...From the Inside Out!*, offers this advice for terminating your tolerations.

"Start by making a list of the things you're tolerating at the office and in your work. They can be a cluttered desk, an over-flowing email box, unanswered phone messages, the printer that needs fixing, the proposal you've put off writing, the marketing you've let slide, a demanding customer, the poor performing employee and so much more," she says.

"Write them all down, big and small. Don't hold back. Be specific about what you're putting up with, what or who's bugging you, what distracts you, and what you're neglecting and/or putting off. When you can, also write down what that toleration is costing you, such as new business or a peaceful sleep. Then do whatever it takes to eliminate those tolerations—one by one."

This may seem overwhelming at first, but stick with it. The rewards are worth it. "Begin by eliminating the small ones first to experience immediate success," Sharbuno advises. "Step by step, clear out this mental clutter to create new space and energy for what's most important in your business and enjoy the lighter load."

DIVINE DIRECTIONS

Make room for success. Are you ready to add "award-winning" in front of your name? Install a shelf in your office and picture it overflowing with trophies and other prizes. And don't forget to submit your entries to these competitions, since we all know "you've got to be in it to win it!"

Get Organized

Greg Vetter of Vetter Productivity and the author of *Find It Fast in 5 Seconds: Gaining Control in the Information Age* helps top executives from companies like Starwood Hotels & Resorts Worldwide and CIBA Vision organize their offices. He says the one thing most of them insist on is the right to keep their piles of files on their desks. They tell him that the files should be in sight so they don't forget what needs to be done that day, week or even month. Vetter always responds with this question: "Are you wearing any underwear?" Once they catch their breath, the shocked

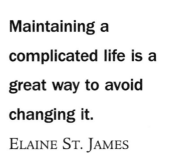

Maintaining a complicated life is a great way to avoid changing it.

ELAINE ST. JAMES

clients reply that they are. Then, Vetter proceeds to remind them that the underwear they are wearing right now most likely came from a drawer that morning. If they were able to find that, they could certainly find their files, tucked away neatly in their desk drawer. Message heard, loud and clear.

According to Vetter, who has a background in industrial psychology, entrepreneurs are notorious for these organizing faux pas, which can be easily remedied with these practices.

1. Your desk is cluttered.

The less you have on your desk, the more focused you will be. "Most people who complain about being interrupted have cluttered desks," Vetter says. Other than your five set items—inbox, outbox, telephone, computer and either your appointment book or PDA—the only other thing on your desk should be the one thing you are working on. Everything else always goes into your inbox first.

"Every time you put a piece of paper down, you're not willing to make a decision about the piece of paper because it will be too uncomfortable or painful," he says. "The next time you feel the urge to unconsciously lay down a piece of paper, take a deep breath and become conscious that you're not willing to make a decision. It's okay if you don't make a decision and put the paper down. What matters is that you become aware of the process. Change occurs only after awareness."

2. You spend your day on reactive tasks, rather than proactive tasks.

Take a Quiet Time (QT) every day at the same time. "QT is an uninterrupted time—about 1½ hours each day—when your door is shut and you are totally disconnected from your email, phone and any other distractions," Vetter advises. "Work on important and impactful tasks, like those you have never had time to work on before. There is absolutely nothing you can do during the day that is more important than this. Nothing!

"Within three months you will be amazed at how much more you will accomplish. Smart administrators know that one hour of QT is worth three to four hours of regular time. They could only dream about an undisturbed hour. Oh, the work they could produce! Yet you have that opportunity—and are probably blowing it. Until now."

3. You keep too much information.

The less you have, the more you will get done. "In most cases, you only use two out of ten pieces of paper in your office. The main reason to save something is because you're going to use it. When you handle a piece of paper and you hear yourself saying words like 'might,' 'what if,' 'you never know' and 'in case of,' you should immediately trash it.

"Make a commitment to go through and clean out everything in your office. Every piece of paper in every file, every book, CD, tape, binder—everything. It might take many small sessions over six months or even a few weekends, but it is definitely worth it. The goal is to touch every item and make a decision on whether to: give it to someone, take action on it, trash it or keep it. Think OATS: **O**utbox, **A**ction, **T**rash, **S**upport. The worst thing you can do is ignore it and let it sit there and get bigger and bigger each year.

"Here are some questions to ask while you are enjoying this most entertaining of all possible activities. Is the information on my computer? (Why have a duplicate?) Have I looked at it this year? (Is the paper starting to parch?) Will or can someone keep this for me? (That's often an overlooked option.) Can I store this in the central or departmental file? (Let the lawyers or accountants worry about it.) Does my retention schedule require that it be saved? (If not, off it goes!) Do the same thing with your computer files.

"All that extra stuff is weighing you down, both mentally and energetically," he says. "Think about your office and the amount of garbage you have in it. How much more focused would you be if you got rid of most of it?"

A place for everything, everything in its place.

BENJAMIN FRANKLIN

If all of Vetter's advice seems too much to take on, commit to make at least one change and that will lead to others. By staying aware, setting up simple systems we can follow and developing helpful habits, we determine what we keep, read, watch, hear, work on and learn from. Otherwise, we become a slave to the clutter. It's our choice.

Divine Aha's

P R I N C I P L E 4
CLEAN OUT THE CLUTTER: THE UNIVERSE
WILL FILL THE VACUUM

◆ There is a universal law with the same integrity and
power as gravity and fire. It states that the universe
abhors a vacuum. When you open up space, the
universe will fill it with what serves your highest good.

◆ You can't afford to indulge in physical and emotional
clutter. Once you recognize the time, money,
attention and energy that it wastes, you will begin to
make changes.

◆ By committing to make at least one change each
week, whether it's terminating a toleration or
establishing a daily Quiet Time at work, you will be
led to make other changes.

Stay Present: That's Where the Gifts Are

Finish each day and be done with it. You have done what you could; some blunders and absurdities no doubt crept in; forget them as soon as you can. Tomorrow is a new day; begin it serenely and with too high a spirit to be encumbered with your old nonsense.

RALPH WALDO EMERSON

How often have you squandered your time and energy by fixating on the past or worrying about the future? By learning how to truly forgive others and yourself, you no longer need to carry the heavy burden of grudges and regrets. It could be the former boss you believe sabotaged your success or the prospective client who took your good ideas and implemented them without you. Maybe you are still figuratively kicking yourself for stumbling through a client presentation last month because you didn't adequately prepare for it.

When you live fully in the present, you harness a new level of energy and enthusiasm and can nurture what really matters to you, your clients and the people who work with you. As a special bonus, you will begin to notice, appreciate and be inspired by everyday miracles that have alluded you before.

◆

Here is a mental treatment guaranteed to cure every ill that flesh is heir to: sit for half an hour every night and mentally forgive everyone against whom you have any ill will or antipathy.

CHARLES FILLMORE

◆

Forgiveness

In his book, *Radical Forgiveness: Making Room for the Miracle*, author Colin Tipping explains that in order to fully release the past and appreciate the present, we must recognize that life is divinely guided. It's unfolding for each of us exactly how it needs to unfold for our highest good. We are here to surrender to the flow of life and to learn that, ultimately, there is nothing to forgive.

How do you resonate with that philosophy? Do you tend to hold on relentlessly to perceived wrongs done to you or do you find the gifts in even the deepest disappointments? We've all heard the adage that refusing to forgive someone is like taking poison and wishing your enemy would die. Forgiveness is not about the other person. Forgiveness is a gift we give to ourselves.

According to Tipping, there are four steps to Radical Forgiveness. First, recognize that you have created this circumstance for your own healing. See this as a good thing, without any guilt or blame. Second, allow yourself to feel judgments, and love yourself anyway. Third, choose to see the perfection, surrendering to whatever the Divine Plan might be. Finally, choose the power of peace.

Life is not fair; get used to it.

BILL GATES

Think of how much more you can accomplish in your life and how much lighter your energy could be without resentment and anger. Each encounter has led you to where you are today and made you better for it. As Maya Angelou reminds us, "To fly we have to have resistance."

Acclaimed 18th century poet and critic Alexander Pope got it right when he said, "To err is human, to forgive, divine."

Practice Momentous Living

"One of the expressions of Western over-reliance on technology can be seen in the lack of patience in industrial society," says the Dalai Lama, whose religion is kindness. "When you deal with technology, everything happens at the touch of a button. This conditions you to become so impatient that when you have an emotional or personal crisis, you don't allow time for the solution to take effect. This leads to all sorts of rash responses, like quarrels, fights and so on."

> Do not dwell in the past, do not dream of the future, concentrate the mind on the present moment.
>
> BUDDHA

Slow down. Resist the temptation to feel like you need to know everything. Take some time each day to experience awe. Rumi, the 13th century Sufi poet and mystic, advised, "Sell your cleverness and purchase bewilderment."

"You can't stop the waves, but you can learn how to surf," counsels Jon Kabat-Zinn, who first shared the transformational concept of mindfulness in his book, *Wherever You Go, There You Are: Mindfulness Meditation in Everyday Life*. As the founder of the innovative Stress Reduction Clinic at the University of Massachusetts Medical School, he brought Zen meditation into the mainstream of American medicine through Mindfulness-Based Stress Reduction (MBSR) programs.

"Use your senses fully," advises Eckhart Tolle, author of *The Power of Now*. "Be where you are. Look around. Just look, don't interpret. See the light, shapes, colors, textures. Be aware of the silent presence of each thing. Be aware of the space that allows everything to be. Listen to the sounds; don't judge them. Listen to the silence underneath the sounds. Touch something—anything—and feel and acknowledge its Being."

How can we be more mindful in our work? I'm sure I'm not the only one guilty of talking on the phone with clients or colleagues while checking email. You may have even been caught occasionally when you zoned out from your conversation, only to be startled by that person asking what you thought of something you didn't even hear. Resist the temptation to multitask all the time and instead focus your full attention and all your senses on the task at that moment. Practice momentous living. Sounds easier than it is. Let's begin with something simple.

The next time you sit down to lunch, say to yourself, "At this moment, I am focusing on eating lunch." Engage all of your senses: appreciating what that sandwich looks, smells, feels, sounds and tastes like. Can you hear the crunchy bread and smell the pungent mustard? Just like in meditation, when other thoughts come to mind, acknowledge them and picture them floating away like a bubble. Practice momentous living the next time you go for a walk. Notice how your

> ◆
> **Let us not look back in anger, or forward in fear, but around in awareness.**
>
> JAMES THURBER
> ◆

feet make contact with the ground and how your arms rhythmically move with your legs. Hear your breath quicken and feel your skin moisten as the pace picks up. Take in your surroundings as you pass a colorful garden or the playful puppy of a neighbor walking by. Stay in the moment of your walk.

Buddhists refer to this as seeing with a beginner's mind. Use the "at this moment" approach while consulting with a client, analyzing an operational challenge or interviewing a new vendor. A bank executive begins each meeting by ringing a Tibetan meditation bell, reminding everyone to listen mindfully and speak honestly. What rituals can you establish?

Being mindful reaps many benefits. You can solve problems faster, show a deeper level of respect for those around you—thereby earning more respect—and reduce the stress you feel from juggling too many things. As the controversial Harvard professor turned spiritual guru Ram Dass put it so succinctly: "Be here now."

Learn from Nature to Go with the Flow

Just as important as learning to stay present, is learning to go with the flow. There are natural shifts in energy within all aspects of life, including relationships, health and business matters. When you are aware of and accept these ebbs and flows, you can use them to your advantage.

For example, when business slows down, instead of going into panic mode or choosing to work with clients who are less than ideal, take that opportunity to work within the business to prepare for the inevitable upswing. This is a good time to clean out files, update databases, and reconnect with old clients and valued referral sources.

Nature is one of our greatest teachers. Look to it for examples of the mission-critical qualities and skills you need to develop. Consider the *patience* of a seed, the *persistence* of a river, the *freedom* of a bird in flight, the *creative expression* of brilliant tropical fish, the *adaptation* of an orchid and the *pure joy* of your dog.

> What I dream of is an art of balance, of purity and serenity devoid of troubling or depressing subject matter—a soothing, calming influence on the mind, rather like a good armchair which provides relaxation from physical fatigue.
>
> HENRI MATISSE

Seek Balance at Work

The Chinese believe that all things in nature are interconnected and seek a balance. Energy or chi is in everything and flows all around us. You can enhance your workplace through Feng Shui (pronounced FUNG shway), the 3,000-year-old Chinese art of arranging your surroundings to attract positive energy, prosperity and harmony. Feng Shui means wind and water.

A business consultant introduced me to Feng Shui in the early 1990s. While I had never heard of it before, I was intrigued when she explained the benefits. Greater productivity. A more peaceful environment. Increased abundance. Sounds good to me! She assessed my home office and suggested a few simple changes that have made a big difference.

Since then, I have consulted with two other Feng Shui experts and read several books like *The Western Guide to Feng Shui* by Terah Kathryn Collins to continue to fine tune my environment. I believe Feng Shui has helped me attract better clients and get more done in less time— so I have more time to play. It has also given me a greater appreciation for the joy of sharing my gifts with others.

Real wealth is ideas plus energy.

RICHARD BUCKMINSTER FULLER

As I explain some of the changes I've made, think about what you can do to enhance your own office through Feng

Shui. To me, Feng Shui recommendations fall into one of three categories: practical, aesthetic and symbolic.

Since being startled is considered bad Feng Shui, you should never have your back to the door. I turned my desk around 180 degrees so I could face the door and be in what is considered "the power position." Water is a symbol of abundance. (Maybe that's why we get some of our best ideas in the shower!) I added a 30-gallon salt-water fish tank to the right of my computer, so I can gaze at the water and the colorful fish within it when I am working. The bubbling sound and light reflecting through the water enhance the experience.

I hung a crystal at one window. On sunny afternoons, I am treated to a prismatic display of miniature rainbows along my walls and floor and on my desk. At the other window, I hung a simple wind chime. With the help of a soft breeze, the chime emits a relaxing, tinkling sound that serves to block out the other noises in my suburban neighborhood.

If there's only one Feng Shui principle you embrace, I recommend that you commit to cleaning out your clutter. (See more in principle four.) Throw out the garbage, file your papers and keep most of your work tools—like scissors, stapler and tape—in a drawer instead of on your desk. You'll be amazed at how much clearer you will think when your workspace is clear. It will be so much easier to stay present without the distractions.

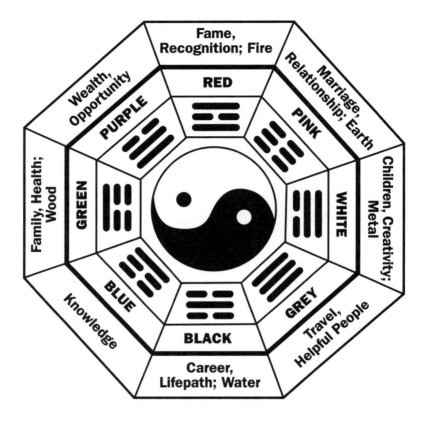

Bagua Map

A Bagua Map is an essential Feng Shui tool. It's an eight-sided diagram that sections off parts of a home, room or even a desktop. The idea is to honor these eight elements or treasures of your life, thereby welcoming more in. Each element has a corresponding color. The career side is always the wall with the entrance to the room.

These are some of the ways I honored my treasures. On the career wall, which is the one I face as I sit at my desk, I hung a Treasure Map. It's a large corkboard filled with odds and ends regarding my top goal at this time: writing *Divine Wisdom at Work.*™ The board includes a mock-up of my book cover and bookmark, a color publicity headshot and an illustration of a child sitting on a hill watching the sunrise accompanied by the words, "Inquire Within."

Just like the book, my Treasure Map was a work in progress that I kept adding to whenever I was inspired to do so. Before the book Treasure Map, I created one to support my family's goal of owning a vacation home by the beach. I pictured it as the perfect environment to write my book. Within six months of creating that map, we bought our home in Gulf Shores, Alabama.

Directly across from the career wall is the wall of fame and recognition. On the credenza are a red cloth runner, three colorful lighted art glass globes and my framed Life Purpose Statement: *Through support and by example, I inspire others to follow their dreams and live joyfully on purpose.*

To the left of that is the wealth corner, which features a healthy, green jade plant and a framed twenty dollar bill. A supportive, enthusiastic client gave it to me the day I told him I planned to write a book. "I just bought your first copy," he said. It's good to surround yourself with people who believe in you—and demonstrate it.

The Five Elements

In nature, there are five elements: wood, fire, earth, metal and water. "Each element has different properties and together they create a balanced environment," explains Feng Shui consultant Jenna Boyd, the owner of Elements of Harmony Feng Shui.

Boyd shares these tips to incorporate the five elements into your workspace:

1. Wood, like a tree with tall branches, represents vision, intuition and initiation. Healthy plants, the colors of green and blue, and the shape of the column bring in the wood element.

2. Fire represents light and brings enthusiasm and vigor. Good lighting, candles, red accents and the shape of the triangle are ways to demonstrate the fire element. The key to a productive office is ample lighting. Add desk lamps and use full-spectrum bulbs, instead of conventional fluorescents. Always open the blinds and bring in as much natural light as possible.

3. Earth has qualities of stability, nourishment and foundation. Use items made of earth or pottery, rugs and the shape of the square, along with the color of earth tones, like brown, brick reds or deep yellows. Add the earth element to the center of your office to stay grounded and centered.

4. Metal keeps the details in line. In the office design, employ simplicity and neutral colors. Any metal substance, pastel colors or the shape of the circle will help maintain balance in an environment.

5. Water is about flow. Bring in water with a water fountain, fish tank or other water feature. Even artwork with water that flows into the office can do the job.

Depending on how deep you decide to go, Feng Shui can be complex and intimidating. My advice is to have fun with it, experiment and use your intuition to guide you. Take the time to feel the difference, monitor the results and continue to fine tune it. Feng Shui will serve to keep you present and make you more sensitive to all aspects of your environment.

DIVINE DIRECTIONS

Further enhance your office. Consider using aromatherapy, such as peppermint candles to energize you in the morning and lavender potpourri to relax you as you wind down from your day. Classical music has been scientifically proven to increase intelligence and I suspect creativity and concentration. I alternate between Mozart for Your Mind and any Karen Drucker CD. It may be Beethoven or The Beatles or both, whatever works for you.

Above all, expect that Feng Shui can help you create a business that is productive, peaceful and prosperous. You are the master of your destiny. Make sure your work environment is conducive to your success.

Catching the Gifts

After we completed a particularly invigorating series of yoga movements, my teacher Julie Wilcox would invite us to "catch the gift" by placing our hands together over our hearts and remaining still for a minute or so. Experiencing this delicious feeling always reminds me to stay present and stop to catch the gifts I can easily miss throughout the day.

What gifts can you catch? A sincere compliment from a grateful client? The completion of an especially challenging assignment? An industry award presented to you by your contemporaries? A comforting hug from your child greeting you after a long day at the office? The warm, soft sand between your toes as you begin a much-deserved vacation? Savor these gifts for they are what make it all worthwhile.

> When we get too caught up in the busyness of the world, we lose connection with one another—and ourselves.
>
> JACK KORNFIELD

Divine Aha's

PRINCIPLE 5
STAY PRESENT:
THAT'S WHERE THE GIFTS ARE

- Resist multitasking and practice momentous living for more productive and rewarding work.

- Observe nature for examples of mission-critical qualities and skills you need to develop.

- Incorporate Feng Shui in your workplace to increase harmony, productivity and prosperity.

- Take time to catch the gifts of a compliment or accomplishment, instead of rushing on to the next task.

Live Your Truth: Time for an Integrity Checkup

Always do right.
This will gratify some people
and astonish the rest.

MARK TWAIN

Most of us would say we act with integrity. We pay our bills and our taxes and we don't cheat on our spouses. When it comes to integrity at work, the little things count too. In the last month, have you made up excuses for not returning phone calls or missing deadlines? Have you ever received an invoice from a vendor that was less than you agreed on and didn't dispute it? Do you inflate figures or results for the sake of a sale? Did you do something wrong to someone and refused to apologize for it? Do you tend to be late for meetings or come unprepared? Have you ever set a goal—a promise to yourself—when you thought you didn't deserve it and, therefore, never achieved it?

> I have found no greater satisfaction than achieving success through honest dealings and strict adherence to the view that, for you to gain, those you deal with should gain as well.
>
> ALAN GREENSPAN

When our thoughts and actions are out of alignment with the truth, we waste precious energy and tarnish our reputation. By increasing your level of integrity in thought, word and deed, you will transform all your relationships, including the one with yourself.

What Do You Value?

Charles Brewer founded Atlanta-based MindSpring Enterprises on his own in early 1994 and, by the end of that year, the company was up to eight people. He took it public two years later and helped grow it into one of the largest Internet service providers in the country. Brewer became legendary for setting the standard of customer care through a clear, compelling set of core values and beliefs.

"At MindSpring, those values were more important than what our line of business was," he says. "We could have been a cheese manufacturer. If you aspire to be different or better than the status quo, the place to focus on is authentic values. Everything builds on them."

MindSpring went national in 1996 when it bought PSI Net's individual subscriber business. Part of the deal was that MindSpring took over a call-center facility in Harrisburg, Pennsylvania. All at once, MindSpring's number of employees and customers nearly doubled and so did its revenue. There was one problem. The employees at the acquired company hated their jobs.

"It was a miserable place to work," Brewer recalls. "There were no core values, and their primary instructions were simply to handle more calls. They were literally answering the phones and hanging up on customers to increase their numbers. It was bad, but we knew that the people working there did not want to do such a lousy job."

So MindSpring sent a "cultural emissary" to Harrisburg to share the core values and beliefs and the MindSpring way of doing things. "Almost immediately, there was an amazing change in the place. The same people, with the same facility, began to deliver superb support. All that really changed was the values and what was expected of them. Within a few months, Harrisburg was equaling or even beating Atlanta on all our measures of quality and quantity. For the people there, it was a really wonderful experience. They loved doing great work! The Harrisburg story is one of my favorite memories of the whole MindSpring experience."

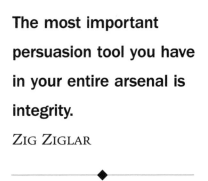

The most important persuasion tool you have in your entire arsenal is integrity.

ZIG ZIGLAR

Brewer warns, "Most people want to accomplish something great with their work and are willing to put in the effort to make that happen. But there is an insidious tendency in organizational life that keeps people from doing that. So you have this paradox with lots of individuals who really want to do great things coming together in organizations that unwittingly make it impossible to do great things. I think the only way to rise above this not-too-impressive status quo is through a focus on the values as the primary foundation of the company."

How can you effectively use core values and beliefs to set a higher standard in your business? Brewer shares this advice:

1. Spread the word. "Once you craft your core values and beliefs, you must write about them, speak about them and hold them up as what you aspire to every day." At MindSpring, these principles were everywhere: posted on the walls, printed on the back of business cards and articulated in Brewer's homey letters emailed to customers. Weekly meetings began with a recitation of them. Each decision was made and communicated with a reference to them.

2. Choose the right people. "At hiring and promotion time, make sure the people you choose live by these values. Leaders who don't believe in and model these values can be deadly to your company." When appropriate, be as selective with clients and vendors.

3. Create mechanisms and metrics that support your values. "Say one of your values is 'respect and trust for the individual.' If you have an extremely detailed policy on travel expenditures and lots of detailed review and checking on expense reports, then those procedures are undermining that value. The actual mechanisms of the company say 'we don't trust you' even though the values statement says we do trust you. At MindSpring, we just asked people to be frugal and they were spectacularly frugal!"

Brewer credits *Good to Great*'s Jim Collins with influencing the way he does business. "Collins and William Lazier wrote a little-known book called *Beyond Entrepreneurship: Turning Your Business into an Enduring Great Company*. They encourage business owners to focus on five dimensions: leadership style; vision, values and corporate culture; strategy; innovation; and tactical excellence. It's simple and short and the most important business book I've ever read."

Following a $4 billion merger with EarthLink in 2000, Brewer soon resigned as chairman and director, selling all his shares in the company. He is now the chairman of Green Street Properties, LLC, a real estate development company he founded in 2001 with two partners. The company focuses on creating "healthy, loveable communities" in urban environments. He's back to eight people and the same core values and beliefs.

Life is a sacred adventure. Every day we encounter signs that point to the active presence of Spirit in the world around us.

Frederic and Mary Ann Brussat

Core Values and Beliefs

- We respect the individual, and believe that individuals who are treated with respect and given responsibility respond by giving their best.

- We require complete honesty and integrity in everything we do.

- We make commitments with care, and then live up to them. In all things, we do what we say we are going to do.

- Work is an important part of life, and it should be fun. Being a good business person does not mean being stuffy and boring.

- We are frugal. We guard and conserve the company's resources with at least the same vigilance that we would use to guard and conserve our own personal resources.

- We insist on giving our best effort in everything we undertake. Furthermore, we see a huge difference between "good mistakes" (best effort, bad result) and "bad mistakes" (sloppiness or lack of effort).

- Clarity in understanding our mission, our goals, and what we expect from each other is critical to our success.

- We are believers in the Golden Rule. In all our dealings we will strive to be friendly and courteous, as well as fair and compassionate.

- We feel a sense of urgency on any matters related to our customers. We own problems and we are always responsive. We are customer driven.

(Green Street Properties, LLC)

Operate by the Golden Rule

Charlie Eitel is the CEO of Simmons Bedding Company, one of the world's largest mattress manufacturers with 22 facilities throughout the United States and Puerto Rico. Established in 1870, the company's annual revenues are approximately $900 million. There are more than 3,000 employees.

Prior to joining Simmons, Eitel served as president and chief operating officer of Interface, Inc. During his six-year tenure, Interface's sales grew from $635 million to $1.3 billion and operating income more than tripled. Interface is a leading global manufacturer of floor coverings and interior fabrics. Eitel is the author of *Eitel Time: Turnaround Secrets* and *Mapping Your Legacy, A Hook It Up Journey*.

> **Golden rule principles are just as necessary for operating a business profitably as are trucks, typewriters or twine.**
>
> J.C. Penney

Eitel believes in operating by the Golden Rule, treating each person the way he wants to be treated. "I have seen big company executives visit manufacturing facilities, quickly walking through and waving like they are running for public office," he says. "When I visit facilities, I always meet with as many individuals as I can, spend time with them, ask questions, listen, write down what they say and learn from them. I follow up with a personal note and usually add them to my Christmas card list. People want to be acknowledged as individuals. It's that simple. I have respect for every job, regardless of status or pay, and that makes a difference.

"The quickest way to halt innovation and growth," Eitel says, "is to blame people within the organization who think outside the box, try something new and fail. It takes courage to do something different, something that has not been done before." Each month, the company presents a CHOICES award to the employee who exemplifies that and serves as a role model for others. The CHOICES award comes from the acronym that encompasses the components of the Simmons culture: Caring, History, Opportunity, Innovation, Customers, Empowerment and Support. "Caring and support are our key core values. It's what allows us to celebrate and learn from our mistakes."

> The magic formula that successful businesses have discovered is to treat customers like guests and employees like people.
>
> TOM PETERS

Miscommunication is one of the biggest mistakes businesses make and Eitel strives to keep communications clear. He prefers face-to-face meetings and a concise agenda. He also doesn't tolerate office politics of any kind. "If people want to play politics, they know their behavior will not be rewarded and they should look to work somewhere else.

"The first boss I ever had was all about power and control and that made such a lasting impression on me," Eitel recalls. "I do all I can to liberate people and to make sure they are happy and prospering.

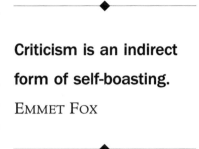

Criticism is an indirect form of self-boasting.

EMMET FOX

Everyone who has ever worked for me and followed this philosophy has made more money than they ever did before." This is proof that the Golden Rule pays off in productivity, profits and the pleasure of knowing that you're doing the right thing.

Get Real

Be honest about what you can't or don't want to do. We all have services that we enjoy performing and, as an added bonus, are also the most profitable for us. And then there are other things we are asked to do that we struggle through. They can cause resentment and negative energy and result in a sub-stellar outcome. No one wins. These are the ones we should either eliminate or delegate to others.

Though I offer a full range of marketing services, from media publicity to promotional writing, what I love to do best is write testimonial quotes and success stories, or case studies. These marketing tools open doors and close deals by selling my clients' products and services through the words of an objective third party—their clients and customers. I make it easy by providing my clients with instructions on how to ask permission to be interviewed and, on the back, a form for them to write down the contact information. I charge a set price per piece so they know what to expect. It's a profitable service that is fun to do since I get to hear how much these companies appreciate and respect my clients and my clients get to see it in writing, which boosts their morale as well as their sales.

I avoid event planning like the plague. There are too many miniscule details and unanticipated variables—like weather and competing activities—that decide the success or failure of a company anniversary party or a holiday open house. Other people live for this kind of work and that's a good thing.

DIVINE
DIRECTIONS

Claim your clients. Do you have a clear, written statement of your ideal client? If you don't, how do you know who to attract and which ones to turn down? First, think of any current or former clients you consider ideal. What attributes do they have in common? It may be that they work in similar industries, possess the same positive qualities (integrity, strong communication skills, and even a good sense of humor) and have the same basic ongoing business needs for the services you most enjoy performing. Second, claim that ideal client in a written statement. Finally, share it with your referral sources. Think of it like a "Wanted" poster and know that if you are specific and enthusiastic in your request, the universe can't help but comply.

Do you ever compromise your values to try to "fit in" or because of "what others might think"? One of my favorite sayings, which I wish I had known when I was a teenager, is: "When you're 20, you worry what other people think about you. When you're 40, you don't care what other people think about you. When you're 60, you realize that other people were never thinking about you at all."

> **Be who you are and say what you feel, because those who mind don't matter, and those who matter don't mind.**
>
> Dr. Seuss

Keep it Simple

Make sure all your written agreements—from contracts to employee policies—are easy to understand, fair, legal (with the least possible legalese and fine print) and enforceable. Clarify the roles and responsibilities of your attorney, accountant and other professional advisors and consultants to prevent misunderstandings.

Model the behavior you desire from others. Though it may be tempting, refrain from indulging in gossip. Its insidious nature can destroy businesses and lives. Remember this bit of wisdom from Eleanor Roosevelt: "Great minds discuss ideas; Average minds discuss events; Small minds discuss people."

In *The Power of Ethical Management*, authors Ken Blanchard, Ph.D., and Norman Vincent Peale offer a simple method to determine whether the decision you are about to make is right or wrong. Ask yourself, "Would you be proud to see your actions from this decision published on the front page of your local newspaper?" Hmmmm.

Four Agreements

In *The Four Agreements: A Toltec Wisdom Book*, shamanic teacher and healer Don Miguel Ruiz shares a personal code of conduct he learned from his Toltec ancestors. The Toltec ruled much of Maya central Mexico from the tenth to twelfth centuries. They were scientists and artists who formed a society to explore and conserve spiritual knowledge and practices. They considered science and spirit

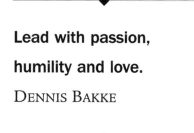

Lead with passion, humility and love.

Dennis Bakke

to be the same since all energy, whether material or ethereal, is derived from the same source and governed by the same universal laws. The Toltec tradition is based upon three masteries: awareness, transformation and intent.

The first agreement is: "Be Impeccable with Your Word." Speak with integrity. Say only what you mean. The second is: "Don't Take Anything Personally." Nothing others do is because of you. What others say and do is a projection of their own reality. The third is: "Don't Make Assumptions." Find the courage to ask questions and to express what you really want. Communicate with others as clearly as you can to avoid misunderstandings, sadness and drama. The fourth is: "Always Do Your Best." Under any circumstances, simply do your best and you will avoid self-judgment, self-abuse and regret. Do you agree?

How Do Others See You?

If you have any doubt about how you are perceived by others, there's nothing more eye-opening than a 360-degree assessment, according to Elizabeth Pagano, coauthor of *The Transparency Edge: How Credibility Can Make or Break You in Business*. She wrote the book with her mother, Barbara Pagano, Ed.S., a leadership advisor and facilitator and the president of Executive Pathways.

> When you see a worthy person, endeavor to emulate him. When you see an unworthy person, then examine your inner self.
>
> CONFUCIUS

IBM was one of the first organizations to implement this type of assessment in the 1970s and continues to use it today. It solicits candid feedback about your professional and personal development with questions that may include: "Do you treat everyone with respect and dignity?" and "Are you honest and ethical in all actions?" Depending on the size and scope of your business, your assessors may be managers, employees, clients or customers, vendors, professional advisors and board members.

The authors cite nine key behaviors that every successful leader uses to gain a transparency edge:

1. being overwhelmingly honest
2. gathering intelligence
3. being composed
4. letting your guard down
5. keeping promises
6. properly handling mistakes
7. delivering bad news well
8. avoiding destructive comments
9. showing others that you care

We all make mistakes, but our true character is determined by how we handle those mistakes. "Even with its inherent risks—such as appearing weak, incompetent or otherwise less than perfect—confessing mistakes signals courage, accountability and humility," Pagano advises. It also makes it safer for others to own up to their blunders.

> **Management is doing things right; leadership is doing the right things.**
>
> PETER DRUCKER

Mission Control

Whether you are a sole proprietor or run a business with employees, it is to your best advantage to invest the time and energy in a Mission Statement. This statement should be in alignment with your life purpose that we covered in principle two. Consider following it with a set of Guiding Principles or Core Values.

A Mission Statement incorporates a purpose (the opportunities or needs in the marketplace), the nature of your business (what you offer to address those opportunities or needs) and the values you bring to the work (competency, accountability, honesty, passion, etc.). It should be inspiring, with proactive, descriptive verbs. Keep it clear and succinct so it's easy to understand and can be repeated from memory.

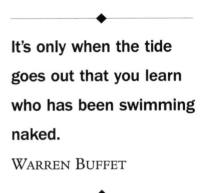

It's only when the tide goes out that you learn who has been swimming naked.

Warren Buffet

Ben & Jerry's product Mission Statement (they have separate economic and social Mission Statements) is: "To make, distribute & sell the finest quality all natural ice cream & euphoric concoctions with a continued commitment to incorporating wholesome, natural ingredients and promoting business practices that respect the Earth and the Environment." Though you may not be in the business of selling ice cream, try to think of a memorable description for what you offer that rivals the delicious distinctiveness of "euphoric concoctions."

You could also follow the lead of these respected companies with a clever mini Mission Statement that reads more like a tag line and is often followed by a list of values.
Merck: "To preserve and improve human life."
3M: "To solve unsolved problems innovatively."
Mary Kay Cosmetics: "To give unlimited opportunities to women."

Walt Disney's Mission Statement is "To make people happy." Can you appreciate the power of this list of values that follows it?

- No cynicism
- Nurturing and promulgation of "wholesome American values"
- Creativity, dreams and imagination
- Fanatical attention to consistency and detail
- Preservation and control of the Disney "magic"

Here's how one corporate executive brought true meaning to the mission. Jim Huling is the CEO of MATRIX Resources, an information technology staffing firm with annual revenues of about $140 million. Through his speaking series, "Choose to Lead Well," Huling shows executive-level audiences how to be their best, personally and professionally. He is a columnist and serves on the board of the Institute for Leadership, Ethics and Character at Kennesaw State University.

"First of all, anyone who attempts to create a meaningful Mission Statement—beyond something the marketing department feels will drive sales—should be commended," Huling says. "It can be very difficult but, if you do it right, there are many payoffs." Some companies will send their leaders off on a three-day golf retreat and ask them to come back with a Mission Statement. The problem with that is they might have a fruitful dialogue of who they are, what they stand for and what they are trying to do but, without input and buy-in from the rest of the company, the statement is hollow and worthless.

> When you discover your mission, you will feel its demand. It will fill you with enthusiasm and a burning desire to get to work on it.
>
> W. CLEMENT STONE

What Huling recommends, instead, is what he did at MATRIX. "We lived through the messy chaos and facilitated a passionate process that involved 200 employees divided into 18 teams. It took 12 full rewrites over nearly 10 months. This was a true grassroots effort with 100 percent involvement. It's a much more arduous process to get to the final product but, in the end, you get there together."

For MATRIX, the Mission Statement, which is called a Declaration of Identity, is: "We connect great people with great people. These relationships result in the finest professional staffing and technology solutions, enhanced careers, fulfilled aspirations and a rich MATRIX heritage." The declaration is followed by a set of six Foundational Values:

1) **Integrity**: We pledge to do the right thing in all circumstances.

2) **Excellence**: We exceed expectations by providing superior service and unsurpassed quality and value.

3) **Respect**: We show care and compassion for all individuals because of our inherent trust and belief in people.

4) **Innovation**: We promote creativity and possess the courage to embrace change.

5) **Fun**: We strive to make MATRIX an irresistible place to work, where fun and professionalism coexist.

6) **Results-Driven**: We believe that our success is ultimately measured by the results we deliver to our customers.

And that's just the beginning. "From the moment you roll it out, you are faced with your second largest challenge: How do you know that it's real? Since any responsible company regularly measures its financial health and productivity, why not measure the integrity of your Mission Statement?" But, how can you measure such intangibles as excellence, respect and innovation? Huling went within to find the answer.

"My inner voice said that in every company I have ever worked for, I knew how we were doing. You can hear what's discussed in the breakroom, see how superiors treat employees and know whether clients are happy." Huling developed an employee survey, which is administered twice a year. Employees are asked to rank, on a scale of one to six, how well the company satisfies each of the six values. Even though it is

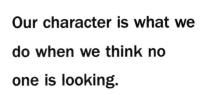

Our character is what we do when we think no one is looking.

H. BROWN JACKSON, JR.

confidential, anonymous and, therefore, voluntary, they often get 100 percent response. The lowest has been 97 percent. The results are strong, with each value scoring at least a five.

But that's not all. They create an oversized "report card" and post it in the lobby of their ten offices. "Can you imagine thumb tacking your college report card to the front of your dorm room door? That takes courage. There is power in public accountability. Our willingness to be scrutinized keeps us strong and, if we ever did dip down in the rating of a particular value, you can be sure that everyone would be motivated to do what it takes to bring it back up." Huling says employees have invited their family members to the office just to show off their "good grades." When MATRIX executives interview talent, they make sure to show them the report card. "When people know they are working for a company that walks its talk, they are finally willing to put their heart and soul into their work. If you create that kind of environment, you'll be astonished at what you can accomplish."

Divine Aha's

PRINCIPLE 6
LIVE YOUR TRUTH:
TIME FOR AN INTEGRITY CHECKUP

◆ Little things at work—like making excuses for not returning phone calls and being late or unprepared for a meeting—waste your energy and tarnish your reputation.

◆ By increasing your level of integrity in thought, word and deed, you will transform all your relationships.

◆ Developing a set of core values and beliefs sets the tone and the expectations for your business.

◆ You can never go wrong by following the Golden Rule.

◆ Get real about what you can and want to do and focus on that.

◆ Take the time and energy to create a meaningful, valid Mission Statement.

Engage the Law of Attraction: Your Thoughts Become Your Reality

---

As a single footstep will not make a path on the earth, so a
single thought will not make a pathway in the mind.
To make a deep physical path, we walk again and again.
To make a deep mental path, we must think over and over
the kind of thoughts we wish to dominate our lives.

HENRY DAVID THOREAU

The Law of Attraction simply states: like energy attracts like energy. Our feelings and emotions, which are called vibrations, have a strong influence on what we attract into our lives. Picture it like the energy of a magnet. Negative or low vibrations, which are dark and heavy and destructive, are governed by fear, shame, anger and doubt. Positive, high vibrations, which are light and uplifting and constructive, come from love, trust and peace. People with high vibrations exude confidence and attract like-minded people.

By consciously adjusting or maintaining your vibration, you will find yourself surrounded by clients, employees, associates, vendors and colleagues who vibrate at that same healthy level.

It's all about the choices you make. "Man has freedom of choice, without which there would be no accountability or responsibility," writes David Hawkins, M.D., Ph.D., in *Power vs. Force: The Hidden Determinants of Human Behavior*. "The ultimate choice, really, is whether to align with a high-energy attractor field or a low-energy field. The same weak attractor patterns that have brought down governments, social movements and entire civilizations routinely destroy organizations and careers as well. One makes one's choice and then takes the consequences."

Lighten Up

"Many people don't allow themselves the luxury of being enthusiastic, light-hearted, inspired, relaxed or happy—especially at work," writes Richard Carlson, Ph.D., in *Don't Sweat the Small Stuff at Work*. "It seems a great number of people are frightened at what a happy demeanor would look like to other people, including coworkers, clients, and employers. The logic is something like this: If they looked happy, others might assume they were satisfied with the status quo and therefore lacking the necessary motivation to excel in their work or go the extra mile."

Carlson says the opposite is true. Happy people are often highly motivated and good listeners with a sharp learning curve. They tend to be very creative, charismatic, easy to be around and good team players. "If you dare to be happy, your life will begin to change immediately. Your life and your work will take on greater significance and will be experienced as an extraordinary adventure."

> I am convinced that there are universal currents of Divine Thought vibrating the ether everywhere and that any who can feel these vibrations is inspired.
>
> RICHARD WAGNER

Raise Your Vibration

We all know people we feel good being around. They're the ones with the positive outlook on life, anticipating success and expressing gratitude for their blessings. They go out of their way—though they would never see it like that—to help and encourage others. These are high-vibration people.

The directions for consciously raising your vibrational energy may sound familiar. They are most likely the same pieces of advice you've heard from your doctor or perhaps your mother or best friend. Your vibration increases each time you choose to love and nurture yourself. Exercise, eat and drink healthy, and get enough sleep. Read inspiring business books and magazines. Be selective about what you watch on television, especially the news. Plan a day at a spa or attend a restorative retreat. Spend time enjoying nature. Express your love. Laugh. Play. Sing. Especially with others. Engage in a fun hobby. Hold a baby. Volunteer. Meditate. Affirm. Visualize. Forgive. Practice random and not-so-random acts of kindness. Give thanks. You get the idea.

"Most of our physical friends are unaccustomed to viewing their lives in terms of vibrations, and they are certainly not accustomed to thinking of themselves as radio transmitters and receivers," writes Esther and Jerry Hicks in *Ask and It Is Given,* based on the teachings of Abraham. "But you do live in a Vibrational Universe, and you are more Energy, Vibration, or Electricity than you realize. Once you allow this new orientation and begin to accept yourself as a Vibrational Being who attracts all the things that come into your experience, then you will begin the delicious journey into Deliberate Creation."

What Are You Focusing On?

What we focus on will expand. It's a universal truth. Cause and effect. You reap what you sow. What goes around, comes around. Unfortunately, we may refrain from expecting too much so we won't be disappointed. When we focus on what we don't want—whether it's another dismal quarter or another challenging client—that's exactly what we create. By "faking it 'til we make it" and acting "as if," we tap into the positive emotions around the success we want and accelerate the manifestation process.

> You are everything that is, your thoughts, your life, your dreams come true. You are everything you choose to be. You are as unlimited as the endless universe.
>
> SHAD HELMSTETTER

Here's how to use the Law of Attraction to manifest a magnificent business. Start with a statement for Deliberate Creation. Write down your desire and the reasons why you want it and should have it. Use positive action words that paint a picture in your mind and make you smile.

Consider this script: "I am delighted to make $100,000 or more every year. This income allows me to expand my business, achieve financial security and indulge in several exciting vacations each year. I deserve this income because I work smart, I perform an important service that benefits many people, my clients love me and I am blissfully fulfilling my life purpose." Craft your statement and fine tune it until it is 100 percent authentic and gives you a thrill each time you say it out loud.

> **Whatever we expect with confidence becomes our own self-fulfilling prophecy.**
> Brian Tracy

Now you're ready for inspired action. Maintain your high vibration and use universal tools like meditation and intuition to tap into the Divine Guidance that will lead the way. If it weren't for visionary men like Henry Ford, we'd all be riding our bikes to work. He said, "Whether you believe you can do a thing or not, you are right." What do you choose to believe?

Breathe deep, clear your mind and take in the wise counsel of Alan Cohen, M.A., the author of myriad best-selling inspirational books, including *A Deep Breath of Life*. Responding to a question on his website about the Law of Attraction, he wrote, "Establish your energy in your goal, and let the Law of Attraction take care of the details. If you believe that you have to do it all yourself with a sense of strain and struggle, you get balled up in the 'how to' of it. But if you launch your intention and stay in the feeling of what you want, life will connect you with the right people and events without a lot of hassles. If there is something you need to do and can do, you will know it. If not, delegate it to the ways of Spirit. There is more help out there for you than you have been tapping into, and you can summon it by thought, prayer, trust, and alignment with your purpose."

"Most entrepreneurs are merely technicians with an entrepreneurial seizure," writes Michael Gerber, author of *The E-Myth* and *The E-Myth Revisited: Why Small Businesses Don't Work and What to Do About It*. "Most entrepreneurs fail because you are working IN your business rather than ON your business. The difference between great people and everyone else is that great people create their lives actively, while everyone else is created by their lives, passively waiting to see where life takes them next. The difference between the two is the difference between living fully and just existing."

DIVINE

DIRECTIONS

Say "Cheese!" Try this ultimate "fake it 'til you make it" exercise. Right now, smile as broadly as you can. Go ahead and stretch those lips. Show those teeth. Release those endorphins. Remember to keep breathing. Keep it up for as long as it takes you to finish this paragraph. Chances are you're already feeling some physiological changes. This one adjustment to your body signals to your brain that you are happy. Feeling better? I thought so. "Flaming enthusiasm, backed up by horse sense and persistence, is the quality that most frequently makes for success," advises Dale Carnegie, author of the classic *How to Win Friends and Influence People.* "If you want to be enthusiastic, act enthusiastic."

Ask and It Shall Be Given to You

In *The Aladdin Factor,* Jack Canfield and Mark Victor Hansen encourage us to embrace abundance by identifying and over-coming our stumbling blocks to asking. These best-selling authors, famous for asking for stories to create their phenomenal *Chicken Soup for the Soul* series, say there are five barriers.

These are:

1) ignorance (not knowing what is available or possible)
2) limiting and inaccurate beliefs (our negative programming)
3) fear (of rejection, looking stupid, endless obligation, etc.)
4) low self esteem (feelings of unworthiness)
5) pride (not wanting to admit we need help)

How many of these can you relate to and how many are you willing to release? I've found a common challenge for many entrepreneurs is asking clients and colleagues to refer business to them. This is true even when they seem to know that they do a good job and their clients are pleased. Start with something small, like asking two of your clients to refer you to someone who they know can benefit from your services, and see what happens. By asking for the business, more money, a better deal, help, advice, referrals or whatever else you need to advance your business goals, you also encourage others to do the same. Each time you ask for help, when appropriate, make a point of asking how you might reciprocate.

Ask Orrin Hudson how he's doing and he'll most likely reply with evangelical fervor, "Best day of my life!" That reflects the positive outlook he taps into as he makes a difference through his work. Hudson, the seventh of thirteen children, grew up in public housing in Birmingham, Alabama. On the wrong path as a teenager, he kept getting in trouble for petty crimes and jumped from foster home to foster home. His brother taught him chess and, later on, a high school teacher became his mentor. He learned that chess is a metaphor for life, and that each move can make or break you.

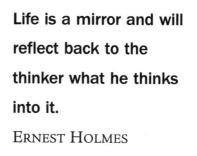

Life is a mirror and will reflect back to the thinker what he thinks into it.

ERNEST HOLMES

Dubbed by CNN as the "Pied Piper of Positivity," Hudson is now a motivational speaker who teaches the game of chess to thousands of students across the United States through his nonprofit organization, Be Someone. "The last words Abraham Lincoln's mother said to him before she died was, 'Be someone.'

He had failed many times before and he took those words all the way to the White House," Hudson says.

"Kids often start out thinking that chess is hard and complicated. Then they learn how to play by following the rules and find out that if they make the right moves, they'll be rewarded." Chess helps develop self esteem, patience, planning skills and concentration. It also builds character. Hudson tells kids that it's the invisible that creates the visible: knowledge, attitude, skills and habits. And never settle for less than they can be. "By being all that God created us to be, we glorify Him."

Hudson often finds strength in Bible passages as he looks for corporate sponsors to expand his reach, with plans to eventually go international. "I am rejection proof," he says. *"Ask and it shall be given you. Seek and you shall find. Knock and it shall be open unto you."* And as we complete our interview, he asks me to include his website address so people can reach him. You may seek more information at www.besomeone.org.

> **Remember, every thought is released as an impulse of energy. The energy carries the qualities, instructions or details of our thoughts, much like our DNA carries the plans to create our form.**
> GHALIL

Judith Sherven, Ph.D. and James Sniechowski, Ph.D. are a husband-and-wife psychology team who focus on relationship dynamics and breaking through resistance to create happy, healthy partnerships. Because everyone is challenged by the differences they encounter in romantic relationships, they named their company The Magic of Differences.

As the best-selling authors of three relationship books: *Be Loved for Who You Really Are*, *The New Intimacy* and *Opening to Love 365 Days a Year*, they have been featured in hundreds of publications including *USA Today*, *Cosmopolitan* and *Family Circle* and they've appeared on over 900 radio and television shows including *Oprah*, *The View* and *CNN*. Success, however, came with a price.

It wasn't until they started working on their fourth book, *The Smart Couple's Guide to the Wedding of Your Dreams*, that they experienced a shift about how to create what they wanted. "We both grew up in lower middle-class families in which most of the men were blue-collar laborers and the women stayed home," says Sherven. "Paying the bills was the extent of their ambitions. I was really young when it became clear that my parents felt annoyed whenever I had to ask for help or even question them about something. I thought their irritation was my fault. Jim's experience was pretty similar. So we each grew up to be overly independent, not wanting to bother anyone, and not wanting to end up feeling obligated to anyone who might help us."

"As we built our careers, and wrote and promoted our books, we assumed it was up to us to create our own success," Sniechowski adds. "We were operating from a 1950s mindset. It was a real effort." So they

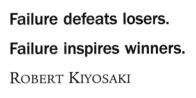

Failure defeats losers.
Failure inspires winners.
ROBERT KIYOSAKI

made a conscious choice to trust that the universe would support them and practiced receiving. "Our early efforts to reach out and ask for help were awkward and self-conscious but we knew we had to do it so people would know how they might provide support. It was a discipline, a practice."

Sniechowski continues, "Kids in grammar school should be learning about the art of asking for help—networking as we call it today—and receiving the help that comes to them. We are all connected. That's an important part of accomplishing anything in life. We've found so much joy in connecting with other people and supporting each other's dreams."

"The beauty of our latest book is that it was born out of trust," says Sherven. "Our editor and publicist were more like fairy godmothers, making sure we chose to use a particular focus. Then, when we asked for help from our email list, dozens and dozens of people wrote to us with their wonderfully touching, humorous stories of unique wedding events—from their engagement through their honeymoon. We felt so supported by larger spiritual forces. Writing the book took on a life of its own.

"Because the wedding couple is so often left to merely repeat what everyone else has done, and they feel anxious about creating an event that would be unique and truly meaningful to them, we expect this book will find a wide-ranging audience of appreciative brides and grooms. This is the only book out there for the wedding couple." With their new divinely guided perspective, they've set a goal of selling at least one million copies—with grace and ease.

"When you do what aligns with your energy, that inner harmony seems to attract others who can help you as you help them," writes Mark Albion, author of *Making a Life, Making a Living.* "That's how dreams come true. Just as they did when you were a child. Remember?"

As you realize just how powerful you are, you begin to take actions that no longer seem like risks to you. "Life is either a daring adventure or nothing," Helen Keller said. "Security does not exist in nature, nor do the children of men as a whole experience it. Avoiding danger is no safer in the long run than exposure."

Finally, brothers, whatever is true, whatever is noble, whatever is right, whatever is pure, whatever is lovely, whatever is admirable— if anything is excellent or praiseworthy—think about such things.

Jesus

Divine Aha's

PRINCIPLE 7
ENGAGE THE LAW OF ATTRACTION:
YOUR THOUGHTS BECOME YOUR REALITY

◆ Like energy attracts like energy.

◆ Negative or low vibrations are destructive and governed by fear and shame.

◆ Positive or high vibrations are constructive and governed by love and trust.

◆ Nurture yourself to increase your vibration and attract more high-vibration people in your working relationships.

◆ Ask for what you want and deserve.

See to Believe: The Power of Visualization

Formulate and stamp indelibly on your mind

a mental picture of yourself as succeeding.

Hold this picture tenaciously. Never permit it to fade.

Your mind will seek to develop the picture.

NORMAN VINCENT PEALE

Every top athlete has harnessed the power of visualization. The runner sees himself breaking through the tape at the finish line. The golfer sees the hole in one. Even my son Connor, just nine at the time and a darn good little leaguer, says he "imaginated" that he would catch the crucial inning-ending fly ball even before it was hit to him in center field. And he did.

What can you "imaginate" or visualize in your business? It might be seeing yourself deliver a dynamic presentation that motivates your audience to buy, sign up, hire you or whatever intention you set. Begin with the end in mind. Visualization creates a space for reality to unfold, just like you pictured it.

DIVINE

DIRECTIONS

Experience the power of visualization. Think about something you love to eat. It might be a hot-fudge sundae with a cherry on top, a pizza with the works, or a sweet, juicy, just-picked peach. Imagine it in front of you. What does it look like, smell like, feel like, taste like? Picture yourself indulging in it. Now, notice what's going on in your mouth. You're salivating, aren't you? Even though you know that this favorite treat is not real, your mind thinks it is and has begun preparing your body for the first stage of digestion. That's powerful.

What Do You See?

Patrice Dickey of The Art of Change is a professional coach and author of *Back to the Garden: Getting from Shadow to Joy*. She taught Dale Carnegie sales training for 15 years. "The most important lesson of all in the entire twelve-week, 50-hour sales course took only twenty minutes," she says. "It was 'Faith Talks' and 'Pep Talks,' a means to access the power of the subconscious mind and guide it to work toward our advantage. It changed my life."

Good business leaders create a vision, articulate the vision, passionately own the vision and relentlessly drive it to completion.

JACK WELCH

She began to read every book she could find on the subconscious mind and the magic of thinking and dreaming big, including Napoleon Hill's *Think and Grow Rich*. In her "Get the Life You Love" corporate seminars and course at Emory Center for Lifelong Learning in Atlanta, Dickey asks participants to try an exercise called Make Your Vision Vivid. "Its purpose is to place you smack into a fabulous 3-D experience by imagining yourself in it. By injecting it with emotion, you make it come to pass more quickly. To bring it alive, use present tense words and incorporate all five senses: sight, sound, smell, taste and touch."

One very sharp woman in her mid-30s, who we'll call Julia, was stumped by the exercise, which was completely out of character for her. She was a successful salesperson for years, and she always knew how to make things happen, especially in her professional life. She worked from her home selling technology warranties at the peak of the high-tech boom. Julia put in long hours to maintain her six-figure income. As they began the Make Your Vision Vivid exercise, she blurted out, "I can honestly say that the only thing that even comes to mind is a swimming pool in my backyard! I have no idea how I'll pay for it. I'm quitting my sales job and going back to grad school. In fact, it seems insane even to think about it."

Dickey encouraged her to release judgment and describe how she felt while enjoying this pool. "Julia wrote it down in present tense, which is very important. We must put ourselves in the moment, since that's all that exists." Julia described herself reclining on a chaise lounge next to the pool, listening to mellow music, sipping a cold drink and chatting with friends. She felt the warmth of the sun and smelled suntan lotion and honeysuckle in the air.

As she described the scene, her face lit up and her eyes softened. The vision represented complete freedom to her. Dickey asked her to experience the degree of gratitude she would feel when this picture became a reality. "Feeling gratitude before the fact sends positive energy into the universe.

Physicists and spiritual leaders have been teaching for a long time that witnesses to any experiment actually alter the nature of its outcome. In other words, by 'witnessing' a positive outcome in advance we strengthen its possibility."

Julia chose to hold on to the vision of her swimming pool and create a new life for herself. Four years later, well on her way to a Ph.D., she celebrated her 40th birthday in her freshly renovated "palazzo" with a swimming pool. How did she manage to afford it? During her graduate studies, she began writing textbooks on English for speakers of other languages. Wisely she chose not to take an hourly rate for her work and instead took a very small percentage of sales, which renders a substantial annual commission.

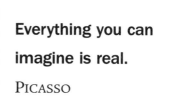

Everything you can imagine is real.

PICASSO

"We sat by her pool sipping a glass of chilled wine," Dickey says, "and she laughed about the fact that it had all started with that seemingly goofy vision exercise. By starting with the end in mind, with a scene that elicits strong, positive emotions, your energy sets in motion the forces that conspire in your favor to bring your vision to fruition. Always affirm 'this or something better.' We don't always know our greatest good."

When Kip Caffey established the Atlanta office of Cary Street Partners, an investment banking and wealth management firm, he needed help envisioning his future. "I didn't even have an office yet, so I decided to start with that," he says. With Dickey's coaching, Caffey pictured all the details of an office, including a desk cluttered with stacks of paperwork that represented three different transactions he was working on. He heard the phone ringing and saw his longtime assistant, Paige, coming in to help him. He could smell the coffee and the distinctive odor of erasable markers.

Six months later, his work environment was almost identical to what he pictured. "I tend to get tangled up in the trees and lose sight of the forest," he says. "Visualization has become an essential planning tool for me. Having a picture in my mind is so much stronger than a list on paper or markings on a board. It sits in my subconscious and takes on a life of its own."

> A vision is not just a picture of what could be; it is an appeal to our better selves, a call to become something more.
>
> ROSABETH MOSS KANTER

Caffey uses visualization to project out six and twelve months. "I'm planning a partners meeting now and I'm picturing who will be there and what role each will play. The number of people in attendance will indicate how many people we're serving and how much revenue is coming in, so I see a very full room."

Take a few minutes before you begin anything important—whether it's speaking in

The soul never thinks without a picture.

ARISTOTLE

public, leading a meeting or cleaning your office—and visualize the entire process and final outcome. If you're interested in promoting your business through media publicity, for example, create a clippings file of how-to articles and profiles featuring businesses similar to yours. Picture your story on those pages with your photo and a headline and lead sentence that captures what makes you newsworthy or unique. If you desire coverage in the *Wall Street Journal*, imagine what your smiling face would look like in a headshot sketch.

Create a Treasure Map

When I began to write this book, I used the *Divine Wisdom at Work*™ principles to create it with grace and ease. When I did hit the occasional roadblock, I recognized it was because I had gotten in the way and was not practicing what I was attempting to teach. As I mentioned in principle five on staying present, I installed a large bulletin board on the wall across from my desk when I began this quest. Little by little, I filled it with messages and reminders about my book.

127

On my Treasure Map, there's a rough mock-up of the book cover and bookmark, printouts of emails from supportive colleagues, an illustration of a child sitting on a hilltop looking at the sunrise with the words "Inquire Within," a clipping from the newspaper that says in big bold letters "Best Seller," and a bumper sticker I picked up from a Buddhist event that proclaims "Loving Kindness is My Religion."

So, what business goals do you want to achieve that can be supported by a Treasure Map? Clip out words and images from magazines and newspapers that illustrate it. Include thoughtful notes from grateful clients. Draw or write your own additions to the map. Have fun with it. Keep it in a prominent place. Review it every day and watch it grow. Claim what you want to attract into your business and let "X" mark the spot.

Divine Aha's

PRINCIPLE 8
SEE TO BELIEVE:
THE POWER OF VISUALIZATION

- Follow the lead of top athletes by visualizing your success.

- Enhance your "picture" with positive emotions and engage all your senses to make it more believable.

- Create a Treasure Map as an evolving visual of an important goal you will accomplish.

Affirm Success: Creating Positive, Powerful Statements

Always bear in mind that your
own resolution to success
is more important than any other one thing.

ABRAHAM LINCOLN

What are you saying to yourself, and to the universe? Chances are good that a lot of the messages going through your mind on a regular basis are negative ones. For many, it's an endless dialogue of: "I won't make any sales today." "I can't survive in this economy." "What I do doesn't make a difference." These messages form a roadblock to your success. Affirmations are strong, positive statements to your subconscious that something is already so. By using affirmations, you pave a smooth road to realizing your dreams. Affirmations and visualizations are a powerful combination, especially when you also tap into the positive emotions surrounding them.

DIVINE DIRECTIONS

Affirm your greatness. "It's the repetition of affirmations that leads to belief. And once that belief becomes a deep conviction, things begin to happen," said the great boxer, Muhammad Ali. Think of how much more you could accomplish if you emphatically affirmed when you awoke, throughout the day and before you slept, "I am the greatest accountant, restauranteur, salesperson, writer, consultant, speaker or business owner." Start today.

Learn to create and use affirmations, detach from the outcome and trust in the process. For can-do entrepreneurs who are used to making things happen, detaching from the outcome can be a challenge. Just remember, the universe will handle the details.

"When we create something, we always create it first in a thought form," writes Shakti Gawain, a pioneer in the field of personal growth and the author of *Creating True Prosperity*. "If we are basically positive in attitude—expecting and envisioning pleasure, satisfaction and happiness—we will attract and create people, situations, and events which conform to our positive expectations." Affirmations help us replace our old, negative "tapes" in our subconscious with new ones that lovingly support our goals and dreams.

When formulating your affirmation, follow the three P's: present, positive and pithy (in other words, brief). You may struggle with using affirmations in the present tense, as if they were already so, since this seems out of integrity. However, the universal principle of affirmations is based on the law that, before it can become real, it must first be created on the inner plane. Trust that this is true. It should always be positive since our minds and the universe have difficulty understanding negative commands. That's why "Abundance is my natural state of being" is much better than "There is no lack in my life."

Here are some work affirmations to consider:

"I love doing my work and am richly rewarded, emotionally and financially."

"I now have enough time, energy, wisdom and money to make all my dreams come true."

"All of my needs and desires are met."

"I am divinely guided to make wise decisions today."

"Every day, in every way, I'm getting better and better."

"We cannot always control our thoughts, but we can control our words, and repetition impresses the subconscious, and we are then master of the situation," wrote Florence Scovel Shinn, an artist and metaphysical teacher whose books include *The Game of Life and How to Play It*. She self-published it back in 1925, a few years before America's Great Depression. "You will be a failure, until you impress the subconscious with the conviction you are a success. This is done by making an affirmation which 'clicks.'"

◆

Affirmation of life is the spiritual act by which man ceases to live unreflectively and begins to devote himself to his life with reverence in order to raise it to its true value.

Albert Schweitzer

◆

Scovel Shinn recounted a student of hers, a businessman who would repeat, "I have a wonderful business, in a wonderful way, and I give wonderful service for wonderful pay." "That afternoon he made a forty-one thousand dollar deal, though there had been no activity in his affairs for months," she wrote. "Every affirmation must be carefully worded and completely 'cover the ground.' For example, I knew a woman, who was in great need, and made a demand for work. She received a great deal of work, but was never paid anything. She now knows to add, 'wonderful service for wonderful pay.'" *Good point.*

Positive Reinforcement

"I attribute much of my success as a business and life coach to the positive statements I make to myself and my clients and those I receive from my clients," says Margo Geller. "During conversations, I use a 'positive sandwich' approach as a way of making sure I start and end with an affirmative statement. This creates positive energy and that's contagious!"

One of the homework assignments Geller gives clients is to write down all the reasons why they are fabulous and amazing people, both personally and professionally. "This is a very powerful exercise and it lights a big fire in them," she says. "When their internal fire dies down, as it will inevitably do at times, they can pull out and review their notes. It's a great way to affirm your unique qualities."

Another exercise is to ask someone who knows you well in your personal and work life what they admire and love about you. "I worked with an attorney who had a feedback session with her administrative assistant," recalls Geller. "When her assistant expressed all the reasons why she loved working with her, such as her passion for what she does and how she is so responsive to her clients, it made my client smile for days! The impact was tremendous, not only for her business but for her personal life as well."

Another of Geller's clients, who is a financial planner, began to ask for feedback from his clients. "He felt so energized and more confident from this exercise that he didn't hesitate that day to pick up the phone and make some important calls he had been avoiding. Each time you get positive feedback, write it down. In essence, you are creating a folder of positive statements and positive energy."

Geller also asks clients to list all their previous successes and accomplishments, going back to childhood. "When did you feel really proud of yourself? Who told you how great you were and what did they say? This includes family members, friends, lovers, teachers and coaches. It's a lot easier to move forward in your business or life when you are feeling confident and good about yourself. Sometimes you just need to remind yourself how special you are."

Write down your affirmations and post them prominently—on your bathroom mirror, the dashboard of your car, your desk or computer. Say them to yourself silently and out loud. If it feels right, energize your affirmations by singing or chanting them.

Affirm What is True

Professional life and business coach Kristi Petersen found the power of affirming success while building her own business. As with many new businesses, each step forward seemed to be accompanied by a step back. "Even though I work with a process called Soul Coaching to help others create positive visions and give thanks despite the outer circumstances, it's sometimes tough to do it when it's your own checkbook," she says, laughing. "But I know the principles work if you work them, so I go back to basics."

She begins by asking herself what is true in this moment. "What is true for me is that I am on purpose. I am here to coach people to reach their potential. I have enough money to pay my bills today. What is true is I have a healthy body, a clear mind, people who love me and believe in me, and the opportunity to build the business I desire."

> **Whatever we plant in our subconscious mind and nourish with repetition and emotion will one day become a reality.**
>
> EARL NIGHTINGALE

Then she turns to the Law of Attraction. "I know it is not my job to attract; it is my job to tap into that attracting force. I also know that while it is fine to 'want' anything and everything, once I 'need' it I have actually become a repelling force.

When I need clients, I am in reality pushing them away because neediness is certainly not an attractive space. I give thanks that I don't have to find these clients; rather, they are looking for me. I affirm that the universe is conspiring to support me in reaching my dreams. I also give up the need to have my business unfold exactly the way I think it should and open myself to the possibility of my dream coming to me in different ways, including returning to corporate life and connecting with the right people there."

As she continues to affirm that she is already successful, that she will never be given a dream without the means of making it come true, and that she doesn't have to push through the details, she begins to feel lighter and more optimistic. "I stay with that feeling, allowing doubts to drift in and then leave when they find out there is no room for them to stay. As soon as I reach that point where I am truly affirming success and coming from a place of wanting and not needing, it never fails that new clients call and are ready to sign up for my coaching services."

For 25 years, Carole O'Connell was a beloved minister who studied, taught and modeled universal principles. As she prepared to retire from ministry, she began to consider what her next role might be. "I knew that the true purpose of life is to live in high joy, appreciating every experience—including the tough ones that cause us to deepen our faith," she says. "I wondered if writing a book about joy was the next step on my path." So she set an intention that, once she had the time to write, she would be shown if a book was in her future.

"Just one month after retirement, my husband and I were on a cruise when my mind began to formulate chapters, ideas and stories for a book. I knew that this was a result of the intention that I set to be shown the highest and best outlet for my energies. My affirmation then became, 'May I be an open channel for wit and wisdom to flow effortlessly into this book.' I have had such fun putting together *Ten Ways to Create a Joyous Life*. I never thought I could enjoy writing," she says with delight. "But, when joy is my purpose, what else would I expect?"

Divine Aha's

PRINCIPLE 9
AFFIRM SUCCESS:
CREATING POSITIVE, POWERFUL STATEMENTS

- Affirmations are brief, positive statements in present tense.

- Use affirmations to "act as if" and attract the people and situations that will help it materialize.

- Write affirmations down, post them and say them out loud throughout the day.

Give Thanks Often: Cultivating an Attitude of Gratitude

Gratitude is not only
the greatest of virtues,
but the parent of all others.

CICERO

Never underestimate the power of gratitude. "Appreciate everything your associates do for your business," said Wal-Mart founder Sam Walton. "Nothing can quite substitute for a few well-chosen, well-timed, sincere words of praise. They're absolutely free and worth a fortune." Giving thanks to others and taking the time to value yourself and count your own blessings on a regular basis serve to open up the channels for more good to flow. Put practices into place that will help you cultivate an attitude of gratitude for a lifetime of blessings.

Stay in Gratitude

A meditator since the 1970s, Gillian Renault has studied Buddhism, Vedanta and many New Age thinkers. She attributes much of her success as an entrepreneur to the spiritual faith and skills acquired from these teachings.

Renault was vice president of communications for a national television network when a layoff led to a leap of faith and she started her own public relations firm. Her former employer became her first client and, over the next seven years, had grown to be 80 percent of her business. With nine full- or part-time employees, Renault Communications handled national public relations campaigns for six of this client's networks and trained talent and executives to tackle tough media interviews.

Then came the rumblings of changes within the organization. "There was nothing definite but I knew I couldn't ignore it," she says. "I meditated on it, asked people questions, intuited what lay between the lines. It was time to start reaching out to get new business."

When she finally got the call that the company was cutting ties with her firm and most of the consultants—effective the end of the month—her first reaction was to shake and cry.

"I was angry. Yes, I knew it was coming; but it's the same feeling you would get at the loss of a loved one who was terminally ill. You are never totally prepared, even though you think you are." Drawing on spiritual teachings, she acknowledged the grief and then started to shift her attitude.

"I asked myself, 'What would Buddha do?' Buddha talked about impermanence. Nothing lasts. This too shall pass. Buddha talked about staying in the present. This client was now in the past. This was the present. Something else would fill the void. Staying in a place of thankfulness was the greatest help to me at that time. I truly felt gratitude for the amazing opportunities this client had given me over the years: Opportunities to create a business, build a terrific team of people, publicize wonderful projects, learn new skills, meet new people."

Renault knew she had attracted this business to her initially, and also knew—on a very deep level—that she wouldn't have to look too far or too hard to bring on new clients. "I already had a few irons in the fire and I knew if I believed in myself and the power of the universe, the work would come to me." The very next day, she received an email from another national television network. "They couldn't commit to the media training we'd discussed a while back, but they wanted to know if we could jump on board immediately to handle a three-month project for them. Yes! This was it." The day after that, a flood of calls and emails arrived. "An existing month-to-month client signed us on for another 16 months. A non-profit client who had seemed too low on cash to give us any more work asked for a multi-faceted proposal."

Then, she got one of those little tests God likes to throw in our paths. "The Department of Defense called offering us several thousand dollars to media-train some high-level military folks, but I had created our ethical boundaries a long time ago. Alcohol, tobacco, pornography and war were among the no-no's." She knew not to take that business.

"I maintained my faith in the laws of the universe and the power for good in this world," she concludes with confidence. "And I am filled with grateful anticipation as I see my company continue to grow and prosper."

Begin a Gratitude Journal

Your gratitude journal may be a gilded book of blank pages or a tattered legal pad. What matters most is that you commit to taking a few minutes at the end of each day to remember and write down what you are most thankful for that day. Consider challenging yourself to make this list a mix of common favorites (My health. My family. The talent and support I need to be my own boss.) and at least one new one (I spoke with everyone I called today. I booked two meetings with prospective clients. I discovered a great website. I enjoyed a beautiful sunset.).

> **Happiness cannot be traveled to, owned, earned, worn or consumed. Happiness is the spiritual experience of living every minute with love, grace and gratitude.**
>
> DENIS WAITLEY

DIVINE DIRECTIONS

Transform your relationships. Think of at least one person at work that you consider (let's say this diplomatically) somewhat difficult. Perhaps he takes all the credit for any success and none of the responsibility when things go awry. Or, she may be excessively demanding and unreasonable. Use the power of gratitude to transform your relationships with these people. Start a separate list of what you most appreciate about them and

> focus on the good, instead of the bad. By changing how you regard and relate to them, you open up the space for them to rise to a higher level of attitude and behavior. Can you see how that differs from complaining about them or offering constructive criticism? All you can do is change your outlook and the rest will follow. Try this one at home to enhance your relationships with family and friends.

Now, think about something that happened a while ago—perhaps an experience you could only view then as a setback or failure—like getting fired or losing out on some business. Does the perspective of time help you see the perfection in this? Examine the lesson learned or appreciate that the door that closed revealed an open window and a much better opportunity. Give thanks and write it down. Over time, revisit your gratitude list. Do you see a common thread regarding what's most important to you? Has that changed through the years?

Pretend that every single person you meet has a sign around his or her neck that says, Make Me Feel Important. Not only will you succeed in sales, you will succeed in life.

MARY KAY ASH

Make a point to send one or more hand-written notes a week to someone you appreciate. It might be a client, employee, colleague, vendor, teacher, mentor or even a competitor. Emails are okay but an old-fashioned note on quality stationery in the mail makes the best impression and often gets posted and remembered.

If you end each year with a list of resolutions for the new year, precede this with a list of successes. By taking the time to recognize your most substantial accomplishments, and the little ones as well, you give thanks to the inner wisdom that helped you get there. The new goals you've set will seem much easier to achieve when you acknowledge you're not doing it alone.

Namaste

Namaste (pronounced NAH mah stay) is an ancient Sanskrit greeting performed by reverently placing your hands in prayer position at heart level, closing your eyes and gently bowing your head. Though there are many variations on the translation, the basic message is: "The light in me greets the light in you." It recognizes and honors our equality and sacred nature.

Express Gratitude through Service

Are you a spiritreneur? Laurie Beth Jones, author of *Jesus, CEO*; *Jesus, Entrepreneur* and several other books in the series, describes spiritreneurs as "those who fully integrate their soul in a workplace enterprise." They want to make a difference and leave a legacy.

Once you get in the habit of appreciating all your blessings, it's only natural to want to share what you have by serving others. As a business owner, there are many ways to serve. Assess what you have to give, including money, services, products, mentoring, volunteer hours and valuable contacts. Choose a worthy recipient, something that elicits your passion. It may be supporting a battered women's shelter, speaking at a business school, funding research on diseases that claimed family members or promoting the arts.

Rita Owens, the publisher of *Atlanta Woman* magazine and former public relations manager for Publix Super Markets, has always appreciated the importance of serving. "I live my life by these words from the Bible, 'For unto whomso-

> The fact that I can plant a seed and it becomes a flower, share a bit of knowledge and it becomes another's, smile at someone and receive a smile in return, are to me continual spiritual exercises.
>
> LEO BUSCAGLIA

ever much is given, of him shall be much required,'" she says. "I am so blessed with knowledge, abilities and resources. It's ingrained in my DNA to find places to serve."

Owens used a personal experience to propel her to make a difference in the lives of children. "In 1997, when I became a single mom with a son and daughter, I looked for a male role model for my son," she remembers. "None of my male friends or business associates was a good fit but I did whatever I could to fill in the gap. That made me think about all the other teenage boys who have neither a mother nor a father to look up to and learn from."

She joined the board of Positive Growth, Inc., a nonprofit organization that, as its mission states, "provides a structured, home-like environment for troubled and/or homeless adolescent males through spiritual, physical, intellectual and emotional guidance." At any one time, there are as many as 30 kids in several homes, ranging in age from six to 18.

"Most of the boys who used to come here were truants but today we see more victims of abuse and neglect—often the sons of crack-addicted parents. They are angry and hostile. Then, they get love and attention and they start to turn around. Our goal is always to place them back with their immediate family or a relative when it is safe to do so."

Owens helps raise funds and works with the founder to use sound business practices to carry on this vision. She began by leading Bible study classes and now coordinates monthly programs with motivating speakers like Atlanta Falcons quarterback Michael Vick. She teaches them social skills and raises their self esteem by taking the boys to black-tie dinners and introducing them to such inspiring leaders as Nelson Mandela.

"They come dressed to these events in their neat green blazers and just about everyone there makes a special point to connect with them." During the last holiday season, the magazine "adopted" three boys and fulfilled every wish on their Santa list. Her own holiday table often includes a few boys from the home. A group from her church, who calls themselves "Women on the Path," visits the boys regularly to nurture and encourage them.

"From a business perspective, I find that serving helps me be people-centered, instead of self-centered," she says. "It influences how I speak to my staff and reminds me to be more compassionate with others. It's so easy to go about our busy daily lives and just focus on our own stuff. However, that's not the example that God gave us through His son. He came to this earth and humbled Himself as a servant. We really are our brother's keepers."

For 12 years, Cindy LaFerle was a local journalist and syndicated newspaper columnist in a suburban Detroit community plagued with a homeless problem. She wrote about domestic themes like home and parenting. "At one end of the spectrum, we have gorgeous old homes on tree-lined streets and a vibrant down-

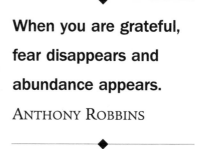

When you are grateful, fear disappears and abundance appears.

ANTHONY ROBBINS

town with four-star restaurants and exclusive boutiques," she says. "At the other end, we have many homeless people who seek shelter in church basements and the local library. It's a perplexing and heartbreaking problem."

She decided to compile a collection of her best columns and essays into a book called *Writing Home*. "It was the week before Thanksgiving when I finished typing the introduction prior to sending it to my editor. I was overcome with feelings of gratitude; not just for my career, but for my home, family and community that had supported me for so many years. I knew right then that my book wasn't about my own success as a journalist, but rather it was an appreciation of community. And to fully celebrate that, I needed to give something back."

LaFerle chose to donate a portion of the book's proceeds to homeless organizations. "The amount I contribute is small now, but I see it growing. I also see my book inspiring others to donate to worthy causes. I believe that artists, writers and all creative people have a forum for showing by example how to earn right livelihood, how to give back." And giving back can take on many forms. Since writing can be therapeutic and healing, LaFerle also conducts free writing classes for breast cancer patients.

"We are here to experience love and to serve, to leave this world a better place than we found it," says Don Olexa. His belief is reflected, in part, by the overwhelming consensus of the hundreds of people he and his wife, Thelma, surveyed for the book they are writing. They posed the question: "Why are we here?" "Most people agreed that we are here to serve God and mankind," he says. "Our book, with the working title *What's the Meaning of This? A Handbook of Understanding to Help Us Build a Bridge to Peace,* explores the reasons for and provides a simple, but not easy, solution to the question: 'Why does man continue to wage war on his fellow man?' It's all about appreciating our differences and remembering why we are here."

> We make a living by what we get, but we make a life by what we give.
>
> WINSTON CHURCHILL

This is not what you might expect to hear from a former attorney. Olexa spent 30 years in corporate America as patent counsel handling intellectual property issues, director of mergers and acquisitions, and general manager of several operating divisions. He attended the Advanced Management Program at Harvard University Business School.

At 55, he took early retirement when his wife was diagnosed with a life-threatening disease. "I didn't know how much time she had, but I did know I wanted to spend it with her," he says. They found themselves in a dedicated search for spirituality and healing. Their search was successful; Thelma was healed. With this newfound spiritually centered life, they began to explore their mutual passions for family (which includes 20 grandchildren), friends and travel.

Today they speak about spiritual principles on cruise ships. "We travel all over the world—Hawaii, Australia, Europe, Asia, South America and the South Pacific; meet wonderful people and share what we know to be true." They talk about being on purpose, how to achieve inner peace, and appreciating and attracting abundance. "Since we plan to love and serve for as long as we're here, wherever we are, our life has become a fun-filled holiday."

As we come to the end of *Divine Wisdom at Work*,™ it is my pleasure to thank you for reading this book and being open to the power within you. I see you co-creating a business that is meaningful, prosperous and full of joy. Your example inspires others to do the same. And so on, and so on. Namaste.

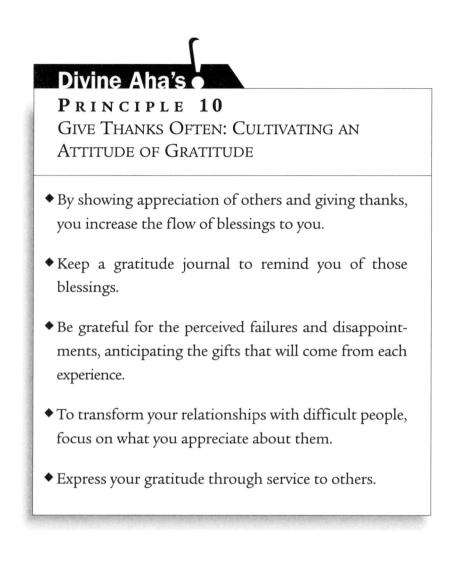

Divine Aha's

PRINCIPLE 10
GIVE THANKS OFTEN: CULTIVATING AN ATTITUDE OF GRATITUDE

- By showing appreciation of others and giving thanks, you increase the flow of blessings to you.

- Keep a gratitude journal to remind you of those blessings.

- Be grateful for the perceived failures and disappointments, anticipating the gifts that will come from each experience.

- To transform your relationships with difficult people, focus on what you appreciate about them.

- Express your gratitude through service to others.

ABOUT THE AUTHOR

Tricia Molloy is a seasoned entrepreneur and business consultant who knows how to work joyfully on purpose. She
started her own marketing and public relations firm in 1988
to support the success of other passionate small-business
owners.

As a New Thought business leader, Tricia applies universal principles to run her company and counsel clients and colleagues. She is also a coach, speaker, workshop leader and
freelance journalist who has written more than a hundred
business profiles and stories for newspapers and magazines.
Divine Wisdom at Work™ is the first in a series of books.

Tricia lives in Atlanta with her husband, Rick Reyer, their
children, Connor and Allyson, and their joyful Golden
Retriever, Honey.

SHARE YOUR *DIVINE WISDOM AT WORK™* STORIES

At www.divinewisdomatwork.com, you are invited to share your own *Divine Wisdom at Work™* stories, ask questions, and offer advice while you learn from others who have put these principles into practice. I look forward to hearing from you!

RESOURCES

For more information and inspiration, check out these resources featured in *Divine Wisdom at Work*™:

Mark Albion—www.makingalife.com

Wendy Y. Bailey—www.wendyybailey.biz

Dennis Bakke—www.dennisbakke.com

Sarah Ban Breathnach—www.simpleabundance.com

Ken Blanchard—www.kenblanchard.com

Laurence Boldt—www.empoweryou.com

Joan Borysenko—www.joanborysenko.com

Jenna Boyd—www.elementsofharmony.com

Frederic and Mary Ann Brussat
www.spiritualityhealth.com and www.newmorningtv.tv

Julia Cameron—www.theartistsway.com

Joseph Campbell—www.jcf.org

Jack Canfield—www.jackcanfield.com

Richard Carlson—www.dontsweat.com

Dale Carnegie—www.dalecarnegie.com

Deepak Chopra—www.chopra.com

Joe Cirillo—www.joecirillo.com

Alan Cohen—www.alancohen.com

Jim Collins—www.jimcollins.com

Terah Kathryn Collins—www.wsfs.com

Stephen R. Covey—www.stephencovey.com

Ram Dass—www.ramdass.com

Lauriann Davies—www.clutterologist.com

Monique A. Dearth—www.incitestrategiesinc.com

Patrice Dickey—www.artofchange.org

Karen Drucker—www.karendrucker.com

Peter Drucker—www.peter-drucker.com

Wayne Dyer—www.drwaynedyer.com

T. Harv Eker —www.tharveker.com

Debbie Ford—www.debbieford.com

Shakti Gawain—www.shaktigawain.com

Margo Geller—margo@margogeller.com

Michael Gerber—www.e-myth.com

Ghalil—www.professionaldreamer.com

Malcolm Gladwell—www.gladwell.com

Jean-Marie Hamel—www.jeanmariehamel.com

Mark Victor Hansen—www.markvictorhansen.com

David Hawkins—www.veritaspub.com

Louise Hay—www.louisehay.com

Tanis Helliwell—www.tanishelliwell.com

Shad Helmstetter—www.whoareyoureally.com

Esther and Jerry Hicks—www.abraham-hicks.com

Napoleon Hill—www.naphill.org

Jean Houston—www.jeanhouston.org

Orrin Hudson—www.besomeone.org

Jim Huling—www.jimhuling.com

Brian Johnson—www.thinkarete.com and www.zaadz.com

Laurie Beth Jones—www.lauriebethjones.com

Jon Kabat-Zinn—www.jonkabat-zinn.com

Cindy LaFerle—www.laferle.com

Og Mandino—www.ogmandino.com

Tom Morris—www.morrisinstitute.com

Mary Manin Morrissey—www.marymaninmorrissey.com

John Naisbitt—www.naisbitt.com

Maria Nemeth—www.marianemeth.com

Earl Nightingale—www.earlnightingale.com

Carole O'Connell—www.caroleoconnell.com

Suze Orman—www.suzeorman.com

Barbara and Elizabeth Pagano—www.transparencyedge.com

Arnold Patent—www.arnoldpatent.com

M. Scott Peck—www.mscottpeck.com

Tom Peters—www.tompeters.com

Kristi Petersen—www.kristipetersen.com

James Redfield—www.celestinevision.com

Gillian Renault—www.renaultpr.com

Cheryl Richardson—www.cherylrichardson.com

Anthony Robbins—www.anthonyrobbins.com

Don Miguel Ruiz—www.miguelruiz.com

SQuire Rushnell—www.whengodwinks.com

Martin Seligman—www.authentichappiness.org

Jeanne Sharbuno—www.focusonethics.com/52ways.html

Judith Sherven and Jim Sniechowski—www.judithandjim.com

Jean Slatter—www.jeanslatter.com

José Stevens—www.powerpathseminars.com

Jeremy Taylor—www.jeremytaylor.com

Colin Tipping—www.radicalforgiveness.com

Eckhart Tolle—www.eckharttolle.com

Brian Tracy—www.briantracy.com

United Church of Religious Science—
www.religiousscience.org

Unity—www.unityonline.org

Unity North Atlanta Church—www.unitynorth.org

Greg Vetter—www.vetterproductivity.com

Denis Waitley—www.waitley.com

Don Whitney—www.worldchildrenscenter.org and www.corpsports.com

Marianne Williamson—www.marianne.com

Oprah Winfrey—www.oprah.com

Zig Ziglar—www.zigziglar.com

Gary Zukav—www.zukav.com

V

vacuum, 51-52

values, 14, 30, 32, 34, 83-87, 92

Vetter, Greg, 57-61

VIA Signature Strength test, 30

vibrations, 106-09

visualization, 121-29

W

Wagner, Richard, 107

Waitley, Denis, 147

Wal-Mart, 144

Walt Disney, 97

Walton, Sam, 144

Welch, Jack, 123

Whitney, Don, 24-27

Wilcox, Julie, 78

Williamson, Marianne, xiii

Winfrey, Oprah, 23

World Children's Center, 26

Z

Zaadz, 31

Ziglar, Zig, 84

Zukav, Gary, 16